THE SCOUT'S LARGE GROUPS COOKBOOK

TIM AND CHRISTINE CONNERS

FALCONGUIDES

GUILFORD, CONNECTICUT
HELENA, MONTANA

AN IMPRINT OF GLOBE PEQUOT PRESS

FALCONGUIDES®

FalconGuides is an imprint of Globe Pequot Press.

Falcon, FalconGuides, and Outfit Your Mind are registered trademarks of
Morris Book Publishing, LLC.

Text design: Sheryl P. Kober
Project editor: Julie Marsh
Layout: Mary Ballachino

Library of Congress Cataloging-in-Publication Data is available on file.

ISBN 978-0-7627-7911-6

Printed in the United States of America

10 9 8 7 6 5 4 3 2 1

CONTENTS

DEDICATION

For Mr. David Fowler, Scoutmaster of Coastal Empire Council's Troop 340, whose faithful commitment to Scouting has set our sons firmly on the path to Eagle.

BENEDICTION

And they continued steadfastly in the apostles' doctrine and fellowship, in the breaking of bread, and in prayers.

—Acts 2:42 (NKJV)

ACKNOWLEDGMENTS

To the dozens of Scout leaders from across the country who once again answered our call for recipes, tips, and suggestions, you have our ongoing gratitude and admiration. When it comes to the problem of feeding the masses, there is no doubt that Scouters have the solution. We'd like to especially recognize the talents and contributions of Jason Cagle of North Florida Council's Troop 169 and Beverly Jo Antonini of Mountaineer Area Council's Troop 49.

Scott Daniels, now the former managing editor for *Scouting* magazine, cleared the path once again. Max Phelps, director of outdoor sales at Globe Pequot Press, sold the "large" idea. And Jessica Haberman, acquisitions editor at Globe, made it real. Especially to you three, thank you.

To those who assisted with testing, Marlynn Griffin, Ken Harbison, Melissa Moore, and Linda Tinker, you have our sincere appreciation. We're also indebted to our photographers Bruce Eng, Krofton Owen, Tracy Tuttle, and Curt White; but to Scott Simerly, Scoutmaster of Occoneechee Council's Troop 204, we owe a particular debt of gratitude for offering so many of his wonderful photos that convey to the world the fun and fellowship to be found in any large gathering of Scouts.

And, finally, a special thanks to John Forslin, for sharing his experience gleaned while cooking for the hardworking trail crews along the North Country National Scenic Trail.

Introduction

With a long line waiting behind him, the Scout stands motionless, staring at the hot dog on his bun. The boy has downed a lot of dogs in his young life. But this one catches his eye because the manufacturer chose to dye it fluorescent red. The wiener pot is large, filled with dozens of cheap, bobbing logs of mystery meat. Too many, even for the twenty members of the troop.

The odor from the pot jars him, and he realizes that he's holding up the line. So the Scout moves along to the side-dish table, laden with musty bags of corn chips recently rediscovered in the corner of the equipment shed back home. And for dessert? Stale, off-brand cookies out of an enormous package bought at the mega-store. It was the second day of the trip, and the camp food had only grown progressively worse. That fact wasn't lost on the Scouts. By this point, many of them couldn't wait to return home.

The Scoutmaster and his assistants didn't intend to serve disagreeable food. In fact, it was the patrols who created the meal list. They wanted hot dogs, chips, and cookies. But the patrols' menu for this camping trip was weak and repetitive, and in haste, the leaders gathered substandard ingredients. Both failures came together at camp with disappointing results.

A review and cross-check of the patrols' menu by the leaders would have immediately revealed the need for improvement. And had more time been put into building a grocery list appropriate for the size of the group, with adequate funds to go along with it, higher quality and more satisfying foods could have been procured. The common thread here was lack of planning. And with a group of this size, proper planning is even more critical.

The truth is, cooking outdoors for large Scout groups is uniquely challenging for several reasons. First, the outdoor setting creates a bigger work load—before, during, and after the trip. Second, if the food is lousy or the meal is botched, there is often no easy fall-back at camp. Third, the cost of failure goes up with group size as the grocery list becomes more expensive, complicated by the fact that each group member kicked in funds for the food. Finally, the likelihood of failure rises with group size. There are just more opportunities outdoors for mistakes and distractions that could ruin the meal.

All of these challenges can easily be overcome with proper forethought. Take the time to carefully plan and shop for an interesting, appetizing, and varied menu. Easy-to-prepare meals are especially valuable for a large group, but don't choose convenience at the expense of taste and quality. Also, ensure that cooking gear appropriate for the group size will be available, and enlist Scouts and Scouters before arriving in camp to assist with meal preparation and cleanup.

Large-group cooking need not be as boring as cold pita sandwiches . . . SCOTT H. SIMERLY SR.

. . . when kabobs can be ready in minutes. CHRISTINE CONNERS

This book, based on expertise and advice from Scout leaders across the United States, is designed to assist the camp chef in planning and cooking for groups larger than the standard patrol or den. Over one hundred outstanding, easy-to-prepare recipes are enhanced with valuable tips and resources to help build and strengthen basic skills that address the challenges of cooking for large groups of Scouts. With plenty of great ideas for your camping menu and solid advice, failure is no longer an option.

It can be very fulfilling to make a large, hungry crowd happy with your cooking. So dive into these pages and discover the satisfaction that comes from cooking up something awesome in the great outdoors for your own troop or pack.

USING THIS BOOK TO PLAN AND PREPARE YOUR MEALS

The recipes are the foundation of this book and have been arranged to maximize the efficiency of the meal-planning process. Information is plainly presented to allow the reader to quickly judge the merits of a particular recipe while preparing for a Scout camping trip. Each recipe is clearly and logically structured for foolproof preparation once in camp.

The following sections explain the general layout of this cookbook and how the information included can specifically assist with meal planning for your large crowd of Scouts.

Defining a Large Group

When it comes to outdoor cooking for Scouts, what's a "large group" and how is a "large group cookbook" different from other Scout cookbooks?

The definition of "large group" is obviously subjective. But a level of objectivity can be applied when it is used in the context of a typical troop or pack setting, both of which are divided into the smaller subgroups of patrol or den. Many of the recipes found within Scouting are built around serving numbers consistent with the size of a standard patrol: eight Scouts with their attendant adult leaders. This head count is easily serviced with cookware and equipment of modest size,

A large group of Scouts: Occoneechee Council's Troop 204 around the campfire. SCOTT H. SIMERLY SR.

including the venerable 12-inch / 6-quart Dutch oven (which is the key reason why it is the most popular Dutch oven used in Scouting).

With recipes in abundance for patrol-size Scout groups, this book takes it to the next level by covering group sizes and scenarios consistent with entire troops and packs. Most of the recipes in this book span a serving range from 10 to 20 and are easily replicated as required for larger amounts. Some recipes have been included with serving amounts less than 10 because they are particularly easy to replicate and fine-tune to a more exact head count. Several recipes for very large groups are also included; these can be readily scaled down if need be. So consider the recipes in this book to be "troop-class," where multiple Scout patrols or an entire troop or Cub pack can be served.

Recipe Categories

Categorizing recipes is not as easy as it might seem. There are as many ways to organize a cookbook as there are eating styles and preferences. The approach that appears to satisfy most people, and the one used in this book, is to begin by organizing entrées according to the meal category in which they best belong: breakfast, lunch, or dinner. Those recipes that cannot be tagged as "main dish" are grouped into one of four other primary categories: side dishes, breads, snacks and desserts, and drinks.

The lunch category deserves special mention, as which recipes to tag as "lunch" are always tricky for the outdoor cookbook author. This section was constructed around several premises, the overarching one being that the camp chef cooking for large groups will especially seek easier options so Scouts can rapidly move on to scheduled activities in the early afternoon. Therefore, the emphasis is on those recipes that can be quickly prepared, served, and recovered from. Only those recipes with an estimated total preparation time of an hour or less were included in the lunch category. The cook desiring to prepare a more involved meal at midday might also consult the recipes in the dinner section, many of which perform equally well at the noon hour.

Servings

For consistency, serving estimates assume the target audience to be active teenagers on a moderate caloric intake. Serving sizes were adjusted upward as credit for healthier recipes and downward for those with less desirable nutrition. Adjust your estimates according to your specific situation.

It's a straightforward task to multiply recipes as required to meet the needs of a larger group, especially when using Dutch ovens. If more servings are desired, many of the recipes can be scaled up by simply replicating the dish as required. For example, if you need to cook for thirty people, find a recipe that feeds about fifteen using a 14-inch Dutch oven, then bring along a second 14-incher and twice the ingredients to double the amount.

Plenty of soup for a crowd of campers. *TIM CONNERS*

But some recipes do permit a significant increase (or decrease) in the number of servings using the original equipment specified in the recipe. For instance, one that calls for a large cook pot that produces 20 servings might be able to squeeze in several more easily enough just by adding more ingredients to the pot. In many of these cases, the baseline ingredients list will show additional columns of measurements for those ingredients, each column corresponding to larger or smaller serving amounts.

Challenge Level

A three-tier ranking was used to assign a challenge level to each recipe: "easy," "moderate," or "difficult." The decision was based on the preparation and cleanup effort required, the sensitivity of the cooking technique to variation, and the attention to care necessary to avoid injury. Most of the recipes in this book have been tagged as "easy," an important quality especially for large group settings where simplicity is welcome.

Because cooking for large groups is challenging enough, recipes considered "difficult" are purposely few in number. Those that are included are there for two reasons: First, they are superb dishes worthy of the attempt; and second, they are meant to serve as exercises for Scouts and leaders to further hone their skills and creativity.

Preparation Time

Total preparation time under pleasant weather conditions has been estimated for each recipe. Rounded to the nearest quarter-hour, this value includes the time required to prepare the coals (if required) through to serving the dish. It is assumed that the cook will flow the preparation steps in parallel and use assistance whenever possible. For instance, while the coals are starting or water is being brought to a boil, other preparation steps can often be accomplished simultaneously. The recipes are written to best take advantage of this.

Preparation Instructions

Instructions for each recipe include a list of ingredients along with step-by-step directions, each logically grouped and presented in numerical sequence. The use of numerical sequencing in the preparation steps is intended to help the chef stay focused and to assist in the assignment of specific tasks for other Scouts and Scouters. This is especially important for large group settings, where the delegation of tasks is an important component to smooth and successful meal preparation.

The majority of recipes are prepared completely in camp, but some require at-home preparation steps. Those that do clearly indicate so. Ingredient lists have been carefully selected to create less waste of key items.

Heating instructions are clear and consistent and provide high probability of success under a wide range of cooking conditions. For extra precision with Dutch oven recipes, an exact number of standard-size briquettes (coals) is specified for use on the lid and under the oven.

If a specific temperature is required, say, to modify a Dutch oven recipe or to adapt it to a larger or smaller oven, this conversion chart can be used

Coal-Temperature Conversion Chart

Dutch Oven Diameter		325°F	350°F	375°F	400°F	425°F	450°F
8"	Total Briquettes	15	16	17	18	19	20
	On Lid	10	11	11	12	13	14
	Underneath Oven	5	5	6	6	6	6
10"	Total Briquettes	19	21	23	25	27	29
	On Lid	13	14	16	17	18	19
	Underneath Oven	6	7	7	8	9	10
12"	Total Briquettes	23	25	27	29	31	33
	On Lid	16	17	18	19	21	22
	Underneath Oven	7	8	9	10	10	11
14"	Total Briquettes	30	32	34	36	38	40
	On Lid	20	21	22	24	25	26
	Underneath Oven	10	11	12	12	13	14
16"	Total Briquettes	37	39	41	43	45	47
	On Lid	25	26	27	28	29	30
	Underneath Oven	12	13	14	15	16	17

(Column headings: Oven Temperature)

to convert the specified coal count and Dutch oven size back into a temperature value. This chart, based on data from Lodge Manufacturing, is very reliable when cooking with cast-iron stoves in pleasant weather using standard size, high-quality briquettes, fresh from the charcoal starter.

The coal count and distribution sets the temperature in a camp Dutch oven.
TIM CONNERS

Options and Tips

Interesting cooking options are provided for many of the recipes.

Options differ from the main instructions and produce alternate endings to the recipe. Options are shown separately from the main preparation steps.

Likewise, contributors occasionally offered helpful tips to assist the camp cook with purchasing ingredients or preparing the recipe. As with options, tips are listed separately from the main body of the recipe. Recommendations and tips that are more generic or applicable to a wider range of recipes and situations, are grouped separately in the following sections.

Required Equipment

Each recipe includes a list of cooking equipment required at camp. For practicality, not every item required to prepare a recipe is listed. For example, a cooler or refrigeration device is obviously essential for keeping perishable foods safe. It is assumed that one is always available for use. Other gear presumed to be basic equipment in any Scout cook's outdoor kitchen includes:

- Food thermometer
- Measuring cups and spoons
- Can opener
- Cutting and paring knives
- Cutting boards
- Long-handled wooden spoons
- Long-handled ladles
- A food-grade greasing agent, such as vegetable oil
- Serving plates, utensils, cups, and napkins
- Wash basins, scrub pads, dish detergent, and towels
- Hand sanitizer
- Work tables and serving tables
- Heavy barbecue gloves

It is also assumed the cook will have the necessary tools and equipment available for preparing and managing the heat source required for the recipe, such as briquettes, coal-starter, coal tray, tongs, and lid lifter when using a Dutch oven. Once a recipe's equipment necessities go beyond the list of these basics, those requirements are listed with each recipe to head off any surprises in camp.

A Scout camp kitchen in action. SCOTT H. SIMERLY SR.

You'll only need a few oven sizes to prepare any Dutch oven recipe in this book: a 12-inch / 6-quart oven, adequate for most cooking tasks, a deep 14-inch / 10-quart oven for roasting or baking larger items; and a 16-inch / 12-quart oven for pizzas and larger quantities of chili and the like. Camp Dutch ovens of sizes other than these are also available, and while these can be handy when adapting a dish for a different number of servings, they are not required to use this book.

When bowls, skillets, or cooking pots are specified for some recipes, "small," "medium," and "large" are used to approximate the capacity to do the job. Most troops already carry an assortment of sizes for each of these kinds of cooking utensils. By having several sizes of utensils available at camp, and plenty of them, you'll never find yourself in a pickle during food preparation for large groups. If ever in doubt on utensil size requirements, err on the side of larger capacity.

Contributor Information

Rounding out each recipe, you'll find information about the contributors. These are the field experts, the Scout leaders who made the book possible. You'll learn their names, scouting title, place of residence, and the troop or den and council they call home. Many contributors included anecdotes and stories to accompany their recipes. Useful and often humorous, you'll find these at the top of each recipe.

Category System

When planning a menu for the outdoors, five key considerations are typically used when developing a list of candidate recipes for large groups: 1) the equipment available to the cook; 2) the number of people to prepare for; 3) the time that will be available to prepare the meal; 4) the level of skill or resources required to achieve good results; and 5) any special nutrition requirements.

As discussed earlier in this section, recipes are first grouped at top level by meal category, forming the main recipe chapters in the book. But from there, the recipes have been sub-grouped by the number of servings, followed by the estimated preparation time, then by the challenge level, and, finally, by the required cooking method. Number of servings, preparation time, and challenge level are summarized in a prominent box in the sidebar of each recipe, specifically addressing several of the key considerations discussed above.

Finally, an icon system identifying the required cooking method is presented at the top of each recipe as defined in the table on the next page.

With one glance, the icon system provides the cook with a rapid introduction to the primary tools and heat sources required for each recipe. Using the icon system, the chef can move quickly past the recipes that aren't an option. No simple system can perfectly categorize every recipe. For example, some recipes call for the use of a cook pot and a Dutch oven. In cases like these, where more than one icon was an option, we identified the recipe by the technique most critical to the recipe's success.

Supplemental Information for the Camp Cook

Additional information is included in the front and back sections of the book to assist the outdoor chef with the challenge of large-group cooking.

RECIPE ICONS CATEGORY SYSTEM

Dutch oven with coals

Cook pot on camp stove

Frying pan (or skillet) on camp stove

Foil or skewer over flames or in fire pit

Foil, skewer, or other direct heating on grill

No heat source required

An important section on safety highlights the most common risks found in the camp kitchen and what can be done to help reduce the probability of an accident. Be safe. Review this material, especially if you are new to camp cooking.

Hand-in-hand with safety comes skill. An expert camp chef is far less likely to inflict injury or illness to either himself or to his fellow Scouts. A section on basic skills reviews the competences that outdoor chefs should seek to understand and master, with an emphasis from the vantage of cooking for large groups.

For those who have never cooked for a large crowd, a detailed tutorial rounds out the front matter of the book. Based on an easy-to-prepare recipe, every step of the process is detailed, from shopping for ingredients at the grocery store, through preparing the meal in camp, to cleaning up afterward. This is a great launching point for the new camp chef.

The appendices cover a wide variety of helpful reference information, including kitchen measurement conversions, sources of camp cooking equipment, a bibliography of additional books and information on outdoor cooking, and techniques for reducing the environmental impact of camp cooking. Also included is a list of all Boy Scout merit badge requirements related to outdoor cooking that this cookbook can help Scouts to achieve.

Healthy Pairings

Wise choices and moderation are the key to maintaining a reasonably healthy diet in camp. When choosing recipes that lean toward higher fats and sugars, balance your meals with light salads or fresh vegetables. Instead of pairing a heavy entree with a rich dessert, select a lighter after-dinner option, such as fresh fruit. If everyone's favorite decadent dessert is on the menu, choose a less rich dinner to go with it. Avoid serving multiple courses at a meal, which otherwise complicates meal planning and cleanup, especially for large groups, and also contributes to overeating.

Between meals, have plenty of healthy snacks available instead of fatty and sugary cookies and candy. Bananas, oranges, clementines, peaches, nectarines, plums, apples, and carrots are all easy to store and serve to large crowds while in camp. In-shell peanuts and tortilla chips and salsa make for favorite between-meal snacks.

The evidence continues to mount that excessive soda consumption contributes to health complications. Drinks with electrolytes can be appropriate when the weather is warm; but otherwise, make the mainstay cool water or juices with no added sugar, and only serve soda as an occasional treat.

Foil packs are great for steaming vegetables.
CHRISTINE CONNERS

CAMP COOKING SAFETY

Paramount to all Scouting activities is the requirement that we conduct ourselves in a safe and responsible manner at all times and in all places. The camp kitchen presents some of the more significant hazards that a Scout will face during his stay outdoors, and yet the risks there are often taken for granted.

Most people have learned to successfully manage dangers in the home kitchen through caution and experience. But camp cooking presents many new and unique hazards that, if not appreciated and controlled, can cause severe injury or illness. The following information on cooking safety highlights the most common risks found in the camp kitchen and what can be done to help reduce the probability of an accident.

Always have the first aid kit at the ready in camp. *CHRISTINE CONNERS*

While the goal should always be zero accidents, minor injuries, including cuts and burns, are common in the camp kitchen. Keep the first aid kit handy for these. But never acceptable are more serious injuries or food-borne illness. Extreme care and caution should always be used to prevent accidents that would otherwise send your Scouts or Scouters to the doctor or hospital.

Be careful. Searing hot metal can char your skin in an instant. Sharp knifes can go deep into your body before your brain has time to register what is happening. Heavy cast iron dropped on your foot can smash unprotected bones. Harmful bacteria left alive due to improper cooking can leave you so ill that your body barely clings to life.

Learn to respect every step of the cooking process. Always think about what you are about to do and ask yourself, "Is this safe?" If it isn't, or even if you are uncomfortable for reasons you don't understand, trust your instinct. Stop and determine how to do the job better, either by using more appropriate techniques and equipment or by asking others for assistance or advice.

And don't try to mimic the chefs you might see on TV. That fancy speed-chopping might look impressive, but it's dangerous if you don't know what you're doing. Slow down and move methodically. No matter how hungry the Scouts might be, no meal is worth compromising health and well-being.

With care and attention, any cooking risk can be managed to an acceptable level. The following list of guidelines for safety will help you do just that.

Supervision and Assistance

- First and foremost, a responsible adult leader or mature Scout must always carefully supervise the cooking activities of less experienced Scouts, even more so when heat, sharp utensils, or raw meat are involved.
- When cooking for large groups, the work load will increase as will the probability of falling behind schedule. If you find yourself trailing, don't rush to try to catch up. The chances of accident and injury will only increase. And don't be a martyr, suffering silently under the burden. You'll only fatigue yourself all the more quickly. Instead, immediately enlist help from other skilled members of your troop to help get the meal preparation back on track.
- When setting up the camp kitchen for large group cooking, structure the preparation area according to work flow to minimize the chances of your assistants running into either you or each other, especially when carrying sharp knives, hot food, or heavy equipment. Give everyone plenty of room to work.

- Cordon off your cooking zone in an area well removed from the traffic of the group and to the side of the main camp kitchen area. If possible, set up physical barricades using tables, ropes, etc., to keep unauthorized individuals out. At the least, instruct your camp colleagues who aren't assisting in the kitchen to stay out of the area.

Food Poisoning

- Ensure that recipes containing raw meat or eggs are thoroughly cooked. Use a food thermometer to take several readings at various locations throughout the food being prepared. Minimum safe cooking temperatures vary by food type, but 165°F is high enough to kill all common food-borne pathogens. Use this value when in doubt.
- Cold and wet weather can significantly lower the temperature of the heat source and cookware. To compensate, prepare to increase the length of cooking time, or, if using a Dutch oven, the number of coals. Windy weather can have an unpredictable effect on a Dutch oven, the temperature within the oven sometimes becoming uneven. The use of a food thermometer is especially recommended in all cases of adverse weather when cooking raw meat or eggs.
- Care should be taken when handling raw meat or eggs to prevent cross-contamination of other foods such as raw vegetables. When preparing raw meats, cutting surfaces and utensils should be dedicated only to this task or thoroughly washed with detergent prior to use for other purposes. Avoid the mistake of placing just-cooked food into an unwashed bowl or tray used earlier to mix or hold raw meats or eggs.
- In the potential confusion of a large-group setting, with several assistants working together in the camp kitchen, it is important to clearly communicate to the others if work surfaces or utensils are being used to prepare raw meat or eggs. Otherwise, the equipment may be used improperly by others, leading to cross-contamination of the food.

- Raw meat and eggs should be tightly sealed in a container or ziplock bag and placed in a cooler until ready to use. To avoid cross-contamination, keep these items in their own cooler, separate from drinking ice, raw fruits, vegetables, cheese, beverages, or any other items that will not eventually be cooked at high temperature.

Keep your hands clean and sanitized at all times in the camp kitchen. *CHRISTINE CONNERS*

- Sanitize your work area with a good wipe-down both before and after the meal using antibacterial cleaners appropriate for the kitchen.
- Using soap and water or hand sanitizer, thoroughly clean your hands immediately after you've handled raw meat or eggs and before touching any other cooking instruments or ingredients. If you must repeatedly touch raw meat or eggs during preparation, then repeatedly sanitize your hands before handling anything else. Be sure that you and the rest of the kitchen crew are compulsive about this. It's that important.
- All food that could potentially spoil, including leftovers, should be kept on ice in camp. To prolong the life of your ice, store coolers in a shady, cool, secure location, with lids tightly sealed. Covering the coolers with sleeping bags or blankets on a warm day will further insulate them.
- Be sure that any water used for cooking has been properly treated or purified before using. Do not simply assume that any water from a camp spigot is safe to drink. Ask camp officials if you are unsure.

Cuts, Burns, and Broken Bones

- Cutting utensils are inherently dangerous, and it goes without saying that they should be handled with care. It may come as a surprise that dull cutting blades can be more dangerous than sharper instruments. Dull knife blades unintentionally slip much more easily when slicing or chopping, and can quickly end up in the side of your finger instead of the food you're cutting. Keeping cutting blades sharp will help ensure they do what you expect them to do. When slicing and chopping, always keep your hands and fingers from under the blade or from in front of the knife tip. It only takes one nasty cut to really drive home this point.
- Do not share a cutting board at the same time with one of your kitchen colleagues. You may end up injuring each other. Instead, take turns using the cutting board, or, better yet, find a second board to use.
- Extreme care should be taken when cleaning and storing sharp kitchen instruments. A knife at the bottom of a wash basin filled with soapy or dirty water is a potential booby trap for the unlucky dishwasher who doesn't know it's there. So don't leave knives hidden in soapy water. Same holds true when storing sharp utensils after cleaning. Knives, in particular, should be sheathed in a holder when placed back in storage.
- When using a cook stove to prepare food in a pot or frying pan, be sure that long handles, if any, are turned away from the edge to prevent inadvertently knocking or spilling the hot contents onto your skin.
- Do not use a cook pot or frying pan that is too large for the cook stove. If a pot or pan significantly overhangs the burner grill, it could topple. In this case, switch to a smaller pot or pan (or find a larger stove).
- Never use a flimsy table for cooking. It could buckle under the weight and send the hot stove and food flying. A table used for cooking must be sturdy.

Camp cookware can be heavy and especially dangerous if dropped.
CHRISTINE CONNERS

- Use protective gear, such as heavy leather barbecue gloves, on both hands when handling hot coals or tending a cooking fire. Ensure that the gloves are long enough to protect your forearms. If you fail to regularly use heavy protective gloves in these situations, you are likely to eventually suffer a nasty burn. Closed-top shoes are also required. The top of your bare foot won't quickly forget a red-hot briquette landing snugly between your sandal straps.
- Cast-iron cookware is heavy. But a large Dutch oven or frying pan filled to the brim with hot food is extremely heavy . . . and dangerous. Wear heat-proof gloves and closed-top footwear when handling hot and loaded cast iron. And if the cookware is too heavy for you to safely handle alone, swallow your pride and ask someone for help.
- Cast iron retains heat for a long time after it is removed from the heat. This is a great quality for keeping food warm during mealtime, but it also sets the stage for burn injuries to the unsuspecting. Before moving any cast iron with unprotected hands after the meal, carefully check to be sure the metal has cooled sufficiently. If it hasn't, or if you're unsure, use heat-proof gloves.

Fire Safety

- All cooking must be performed in a fire-safe area of camp, clear of natural combustibles like dry leaves, grass, and trees, and away from wooden structures. When cooking directly on the ground using coals, select a durable area covered in fireproof material such as rock, gravel, or bare earth. Be sure to follow any special open-fire restrictions established for your region. Ask camp officials about this when checking in. Always have a large bucket of water handy to douse any flames that may escape your fire-safe perimeter.

- When using a cook stove, keep loose and combustible items such as dish towels, plastic bags, aprons, long sleeves, and shirts away from the flame.
- Cooking fires require special attention to avoid injury. Keep the fire just large enough to do the job. Use long-handled tongs when managing foods in the fire. If cooking above a fire using a grill grate, ensure that the grate is strong and sturdy enough to handle the weight of the cookware and food that you're placing on it. Be sure the fire is out cold before leaving camp.
- Hot coals on the ground present a potential hazard during cooking, but especially afterward. With a Dutch oven off the heat, and with the coals ashed over, the threat lurking in your cooking area might go unnoticed. Notify your fellow Scouts and Scouters of the danger of hot coals on the ground. Keep the area off-limits to all but essential personnel until the coals expire. Once the coals have fully cooled, discard the ash in a fire-safe manner appropriate for your camp.
- Unless vented, noxious fumes from a camp stove or burning coals will rise and concentrate within the apex of any roof under which cooking is performed. So when a kitchen tent or tarp structure is used for cooking in camp, the apex must be substantially higher than a tall person's head, and with walls open and well ventilated on all sides. When cooking in a kitchen tent, be especially diligent to maintain a large fire-safe perimeter around the cooking area. Never attempt to cook in a sleeping tent, even a large one. The fully enclosed walls will concentrate deadly gases and cause asphyxiation; or the tent floor or walls could rapidly catch fire and trap the occupants. A standard picnic canopy with low ceiling or partially enclosed side walls is also

unsafe for cooking because the apex is at head height and the walls are often too low or poorly ventilated.

- Do not use a barbecue grill in a kitchen tent. Flare-up could create a fire hazard, and any concentration of smoke could be dangerous.

Allergies and Special Diets

- When planning a menu for an outing, ask your fellow Scouts and Scouters if any have food allergies or health issues that might require special dietary restrictions. Selecting recipes that meet everyone's requirements might seem impossible in these circumstances, but many recipes can be modified to meet special dietary requirements while satisfying everyone else in the group. This approach can be far easier on the cook than attempting to adhere to a parallel special-requirements menu.

Wild Animals

- Animals searching for food scraps and garbage can pose a danger to the camp environment either through aggression or disease. Dirty dishes unattended, unsecured garbage, food items and coolers left in the open: These all will eventually attract unwanted animal attention. Wildlife that gains access to such goodies will surely come back for more, placing these animals at risk of harm along with the people who must then interact with them or remove them. A camp that is kept neat and clean, with food and garbage properly and securely stored, is far less attractive to the local fauna. Practice low-impact camping principles and adhere to any food storage regulations unique to your area or camp.
- No list can cover every danger lurking in any situation, and the above is surely no exception. But by learning to cook with a mind fixated on safety, few circumstances will catch you ill-prepared or by surprise.

BASIC SKILLS FOR THE LARGE-GROUP CHEF

"Time is not exactly your enemy. But, mismanaged, it's sure not your friend."

—John Forslin, speaking of his experience as trail crew camp chef, as quoted in The North Star *magazine*

Pleasing a large group of Scouts with your cooking doesn't come by accident. A strong foundation in the fundamentals of outdoor cookery in general and cooking for crowds in particular will make it all the more likely that you'll be successful. With this in mind, the following section covers the essential skills of cooking for large groups.

Planning for the Obvious . . . and the Unexpected

- If you are a camp-cooking neophyte, keep your menu simple, especially when cooking for a large crowd. Raise the challenge level only after you've become more skilled and confident in your abilities. Taking on more work than one can manage is a common camp kitchen mistake, and the botched meal that results is sure to disappoint not only the one doing the work but also the many hungry stomachs depending on the chef.
- Many recipes serve admirably as "one-pot" meals. These are perfect for the large-group setting, where simplicity is critical. Unless you are looking for a real challenge, avoid complex, multicourse meals, and rely instead on a one-pot entree and a simple side or two, such as fresh salad and sliced bread. Aluminum "steam table pans" make excellent and inexpensive containers for serving large quantities of salads and breads to your group.

Gathering the groceries for the next camping trip.

SCOTT H. SIMERLY SR.

- While a simpler menu is often the best approach as group size grows, don't make the mistake of choosing boring, bland, and cheap foods just because they are simple. You'll find plenty of easy and very tasty options in this cookbook that your large group will love.
- Groceries account for the majority of cost on most outings, and parents appreciate when efforts are made to keep camping expenses reasonable. However, cost-cutting can be taken to an extreme, with ingredients of such low quality that it's painfully obvious, meal after meal. Be frugal with other people's money, but be prudent about cost-cutting measures. Spend the extra money when it makes sense. It's justifiable, and the Scouts and Scouters will appreciate the difference.
- The ability to multitask is a hallmark of great chefs, and it becomes even more important when dealing with large quantities of ingredients or when replicating recipes. Don't act as the Lone Ranger when cooking for large groups. Enlist help and divide kitchen duties among Scouts and leaders to lighten the load while cooking and cleaning. Discuss roles and responsibilities in advance so there is no confusion or push-back when it comes time to engage. The recipes in this book use numerical sequencing for the instructions. Use these to best assign tasks to the helpers.
- They are often enthusiastic to help, but younger Scouts can require much more supervision. Make sure you can manage the additional workload when assigning tasks to the tenderfoots. Some don't know a can opener from a pizza cutter or won't have a clue as to how to crack an egg. If cooking for a very large crowd, it may be better to leave the inexperienced chefs out of the kitchen altogether.

- The younger the children, the more they tend to openly grumble about their food, even when it is obviously awesome to everyone else. And after a long evening of cooking in camp, complaining is the last thing you want to hear from the Scouts. A powerful way to avoid this is to include your Scouts, especially the younger ones, in the meal planning process. By giving them a voice, they become stakeholders in the meal's success and are more likely to enjoy, not just tolerate, the results.
- Read through and understand the entire recipe before commencing preparation. You are less likely to make a critical mistake by doing so. And be sure that you have everything needed before starting recipe preparation by first gathering all ingredients and cooking utensils to your work area.
- When planning your menu, don't ignore the flexibility of the camp Dutch oven, which can be used in place of a frying pan, grille grate, or cook pot for many recipes that otherwise require them. If a camp stove, barbecue grill, or wood fire will be unavailable for your favorite recipes at your next outing, consider adapting these dishes to the circumstances. A camp Dutch oven and a bag of briquettes can probably do the job easily and admirably.
- Foul weather adds a powerful variable to the camp cooking equation. And bugs and wild animals further distract by keeping you on the defensive. Prior to any outing,

Younger Scouts engaged in the cooking process are less likely to grumble about the menu. SCOTT H. SIMERLY SR.

weather and critters should be considered and planned for appropriately. Be realistic about what you can handle under the likely circumstances. The more trying the conditions, the simpler the menu should be.

- Even the most foolproof dish sometimes ends its short life tragically dumped in the dirt by fate or accident. Whatever the cause may be, always have a Plan B at the ready, whether it is boxed macaroni or a map to the nearest grocery store. At some point, you and your Scouts are likely to need it.

Tailoring Your Camp Kitchen for a Large Group

- Once arriving at camp, give careful thought to your kitchen area. Set up the tables in a quiet, level corner, if possible. Choose an area with a durable surface. Otherwise, all the foot traffic will wear down grasses and sensitive plant growth. Avoid muddy or low-lying areas, especially if rain is in the forecast. The kitchen must be in a fire-safe area. If using a camp fire or Dutch oven, the cooking area should be adjacent to the camp kitchen so that a close eye can be kept on the situation. When using coals or a campfire, a fire-safe perimeter must be established around the cooking area, free of all combustibles.
- Consider your work flow, and logically position the cooking area, work tables, serving tables, storage bins, coolers, and trash containers to minimize cross-traffic (and collisions) within the kitchen area. If possible, set the serving area away from the main kitchen so that hungry diners don't get in the way of the cooks as they go about finishing their tasks.
- When cooking for large groups, bring along extra mixing bowls and other less expensive utensils, such as knives, measuring cups, and long-handled mixing spoons. That way, all of your assistants will never be without the tools they need to do their job. And always have several cutting boards available. Lack of adequate cutting equipment is a common bottleneck in the camp kitchen.

- Have plenty of sturdy folding tables when cooking for large crowds. Otherwise, if table space is very limited, and some of the food prep is relegated to the serving area or ground, the process can quickly become unhygienic, inefficient, and frustrating. Keep in mind that extra table space will also be required for serving the food.

Reduce, Reuse, Recycle

- Give special attention to servingware for your large group. Avoid waste by setting out only the plates, bowls, and utensils required for the meal. Ask Scouts to reuse their servingware for other courses, such as salad or dessert. Have a permanent marker available for writing names on disposable plastic cups so that these can be reused. Better yet, have Scouts and Scouters use their personal mess kits when possible, or, at the least, bring durable plastic drinking cups from home with their names marked on them.
- Some servingware, though disposable, is robust enough to pass through the dishwasher. If this is the case for your situation, consider using a bin, box, aluminum steam table pan, or bag to collect used utensils once they've been rinsed. Then clean them in bulk at home in the dishwasher for future reuse.

Managing the Heat

- When using a cook pot, skillet, or Dutch oven on a grate over an open fire, the cooking temperature is much easier to control if the flames are low and the fire has a solid bed of embers. If you plan to use open fire as your heat source, start the campfire long before mealtime to give it time to die down and stabilize.
- Foil packets are convenient for cooking many types of foods. But this is one of the more challenging methods for properly controlling temperature and avoiding over- or undercooked foods. When using foil packets, more predictable results can be obtained if the packets

are placed on a grate over a campfire, briquettes, or propane grill as opposed to tossing the foil packets directly onto the embers of a campfire. It's important to use a tight seal to hold in moisture along with a generous air pocket for the contents because the food cooks in part by steaming. Heavy-duty foil is recommended, and if the fire is particularly hot, use two layers, wrapping your food in the first sheet, tightly sealing the edges, then doing the same with the second sheet.

- Select a high-quality briquette of standard size when using charcoal with your Dutch oven. Extra-large or small briquettes, or even embers from the camp fire, can also work, but their non-standard size will make it more challenging to achieve proper results when following a cookbook, such as this one, that specifies exact coal counts based on the standard briquette size.
- Many Dutch oven recipes with a high liquid content, such as stews, can easily tolerate nonexact briquette counts. Because of this, irregular-size coals from the campfire can be readily used as the fuel source instead. By using embers from the campfire, the additional twenty minutes or so otherwise required to start briquettes from scratch is eliminated. Reducing the preparation time in this manner also makes many Dutch oven dinner recipes a viable option at lunchtime, even when the schedule is tight.
- Intense heat is transferred through the walls of a Dutch oven in those areas where coals come into direct contact with the metal. Food touching the walls on the inside surface of these hot spots will likely char. With coals on the lid, it is imperative that tall foods, such as rising breads or roasts, are cooked in a Dutch oven deep enough for the food to avoid contacting the lid's inside surface. And underneath the oven, the briquettes must be positioned to not directly touch the metal's underside. Otherwise food on the floor of the oven will probably burn. If these simple rules are followed, you should never find it necessary to scrape carbon from your breads or expensive cuts of meat.

- Briquettes often clump together when placing or moving the oven during cooking. They sometimes congregate on the lid, but their sly gatherings usually occur under the oven, where they are more difficult to observe. The problem with this unruly behavior is that it can create hot spots that produce uneven cooking, especially while baking. To prevent this, redistribute the wayward coals as necessary, especially under the oven, and rotate the oven one-quarter turn over the briquettes every 15 minutes or so. At the same time, use a lid-lifter to carefully rotate the lid one-quarter turn relative to the base.
- Heat escapes quickly when the lid is raised from a Dutch oven. Tempting as it may be to continually peek at that cake, don't do so unless absolutely necessary. You'll only lengthen the cooking time.
- Hot briquettes quickly fail when used directly on moist surfaces. Avoid this common mistake by placing your coals and oven on a metal tray or other durable, dry, fireproof surface, such as the flat side of a row of cinder blocks. A tray or hard surface prevents the oven from settling down into the soil and onto direct contact with the coals under the oven, which could otherwise cause the food to char. Cooking on a tray or raised surface also protects the ground from scarring and makes ash cleanup and disposal easier once the coals expire.
- Always bring plenty of extra charcoal briquettes to cover contingencies. Food preparation may take longer than expected, requiring additional coals to complete the meal. Windy, cold, or wet weather can also greatly increase the number of coals required. Don't get caught with an empty bag of briquettes and your food half-baked.
- Preheating the Dutch oven is called for in recipes that require hot metal to properly kick-start the cooking process, such as when baking, sautéing vegetables, or browning meats. When browning or sautéing, exact coal count isn't essential for preheating the oven, with about two dozen briquettes generally adequate for the job, and all the coals go under the oven because the lid is unused. When preheating

the oven for recipes requiring the lid, the coals should be distributed between the lid and under the oven. Use any unspent coals for subsequent cooking steps.

- Most recipes for the Dutch oven are remarkably resilient against overcooking. The heavy, tight-fitting lid helps trap moisture, which prevents foods from drying out when left on the coals longer than they need to be. However, as is true in the home kitchen, baked items require more precision for great results. So pay closer attention to temperature and timing when baking.
- When cooking with more than one Dutch oven at mealtime, stacking the ovens, one on top of the other, can be a useful technique if the cooking area is limited. This method also saves on briquettes, as the coals on the lid of the bottom oven also heat the bottom of the oven on top. But be aware that stacking complicates the preparation, requiring careful placement of the ovens and more attention to coal distribution and cooking times. For instance, you wouldn't want to place a dish that requires frequent stirring at the bottom of the stack. Nor would you stack a Dutch oven that uses a low coal count on top of one requiring a lot of briquettes. Stacking several ovens can also be more hazardous, as a taller tower becomes more prone to toppling. Plan carefully and be extra cautious when using stacks.

Dealing with the Weather

- When a coal-covered Dutch oven lid is lifted while the wind is stirring, or if the lid is bumped while lifting, you'll watch in helpless wonder as ash majestically floats down onto your food. It's a beautiful sight, like powdered sugar on a chocolate cake. Unfortunately, ash doesn't taste like powdered sugar. So avoid jarring the lid when lifting, and remove it immediately toward the downwind side. This will minimize your ash-to-food ratio.
- In very windy conditions, place your stove or Dutch oven behind a windscreen of some sort while cooking, otherwise the food will be

subjected to uneven heating, potentially burned in some areas and undercooked in others. A row of coolers or storage bins can serve handily as a windbreak. Dutch oven stands, purpose-built for cooking off the ground, often come with built-in windscreens.

- Chilly or windy weather presents a real challenge to keeping food warm prior to serving. This is especially true when preparing food in batches. Cooked foods can be placed in aluminum steam table trays, covered with foil, then layered in dry dish towels for insulation. A gas grill with a cover is very effective. Even coolers holding a few hot rocks from around the perimeter of the fire can serve as warming ovens provided that the rocks aren't so hot as to melt the plastic.
- Perhaps the most challenging of all outdoor cooking situations in an open kitchen involves rain. Sometimes, the only option is to cease and desist, serving no-cook foods instead, or to move the camp kitchen to a fire-safe covered area.
- When using Dutch ovens in the rain, large sheets of heavy-duty aluminum foil, tented loosely over the top of the oven and tray, can offer some protection in a pinch but are unlikely to shield completely during a cloudburst. A large barbecue grill with a lid can protect your oven from the rain, with a metal tray placed on the grill grate serving as the cook surface. And, once again, a Dutch oven stand with a windscreen would serve nicely, with the screen supporting sheets of heavy foil or a tray for keeping the rain off the coals.

A little rain isn't stopping these camp chefs.
CURT WHITE, AKA THE TITANIUM CHEF

- A camp kitchen tent is arguably the most comfortable option for cooking in wet weather, but good judgment is a must when choosing and using a kitchen tent because of the very real risk of asphyxiation and fire. See the previous section for important information on kitchen tent safety.
- Cooking with a Dutch oven in snow presents it own unique difficulties, but these are easily managed if planned for in advance. If the snow is deep and cannot be easily cleared, cook off the ground on a durable surface. For example, a metal tray on a concrete picnic table would work well in this instance. A Dutch oven stand can also be very useful in the snow. If your camping area has a sturdy grill, a tray placed on the grate can be used. Wood logs can also be arranged in the snow to securely support a metal tray for placing the Dutch oven. The flat surface of several cinder blocks would also work well in this situation.

Cleaning Up

- A pair of large butler basins or storage containers, one filled with sudsy water, the other with rinse water, makes cleanup more efficient.
- When cooking for a large group, it's important to have adequate gear for cleanup. Be sure to have wash and rinse bins of a size large enough for the situation. Even better, set up a second wash-rinse station to speed the process. Ensure that there are plenty of wash rags, scrub pads, and clean towels for the job.
- A lining of heavy-duty foil in the Dutch oven is excellent for containing mess from gooey recipes. Once the foil is removed following the meal, most of the glop goes with it, making cleanup much easier. Note that foil is not suitable for recipes that require a lot of stirring, because the foil can snag and tear.
- Cleaning greasy cookware and dishes with cold water can be a real challenge to one's patience. Use warm water to cut grease and make

cleanup more rapid and hygienic. Place a pot of water over the stove or campfire to warm for this purpose while the meal is being served. The water will be hot once it's time for cleanup. Carefully pour the hot water into the wash bin, bringing it to a safe temperature with cold water as required.

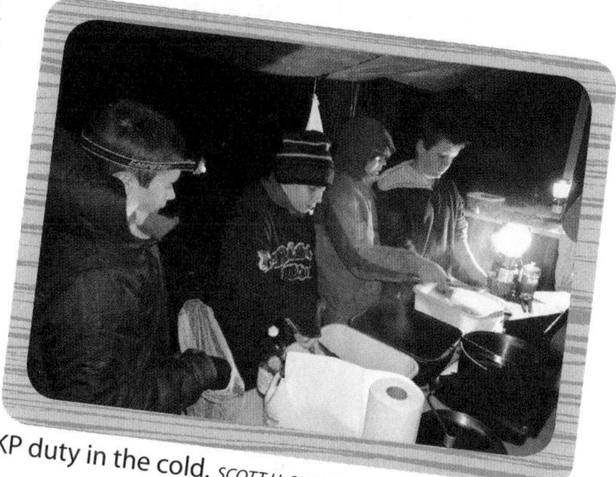

KP duty in the cold. SCOTT H. SIMERLY SR.

- Use dishwashing liquid sparingly during cleanup, just enough to do the job. Only detergents that are biodegradable should be used outdoors. As a general rule, don't use detergents on cast iron. (Information specific to cleaning and storing cast iron can be found in the following section.)
- Dirty dishes left to lie will eventually attract bugs and wild animals. To avoid such interest, ensure that all cookware and utensils have been washed and rinsed before leaving camp during the day or when retiring for the evening.
- Dispose of wash and rinse water, also called "gray water," in a manner acceptable for your particular camp. Some camping areas have dedicated gray water disposal stations. Never dump gray water directly into a stream or lake.

Caring for Cast Iron

- For cleanup, cast-iron cookware requires no more than a sponge or dish rag for wiping, a gentle nonmetallic scrub pad or spatula for scraping, warm water for washing, plenty of clean water for rinsing, and a towel for drying. Metal scouring pads are a sure way to destroy your cast iron's protective coating and should never be used. Detergents should be avoided unless absolutely necessary because soap attacks the cast iron's patina (also called its seasoning).

- The warmer the wash water, the more effectively that grease can be cut by water alone. When grease is heavy or solidified, and the wash water cold, a very small amount of dish soap will make cast-iron cleanup easier. But the outer layer of patina can be compromised in the process. For this reason, use soap sparingly, if ever.
- Never use a dishwasher to clean your cast iron. The strong detergents in a dishwasher can remove so much coating that re-seasoning would be required.
- Some dishes will challenge even the best nonstick coating, especially if the food is frozen when first placed in the cookware, or if the food is accidentally charred while cooking. Soaking cookware in water is the usual remedy for tough stuck-on foods, but cast iron should not be left to soak for long periods in plain water. Otherwise, the patina may weaken and rust spots form. Instead, an effective and non-damaging cleaning method is to pour an inch or two of very hot water into the soiled cookware before the residue has a chance to harden. The stubborn food will begin to loosen after just a few minutes. Once the soak water cools to a safe temperature, the residue can be removed with a nonmetallic spatula or scrub pad and the cookware then cleaned and rinsed as usual.
- If a separate cook pot is unavailable to heat wash water, the soiled Dutch oven or skillet itself can be used by adding a shallow pool of clean water then placing it over the camp fire, camp stove, or any remaining hot coals. Once the water is hot, very carefully move the cast iron to a safe location. Once the metal cools to a temperature safe for cleaning, the food residue will have loosened and subsequent cleanup will be much easier.

- When cleaning or drying, never allow cast-iron cookware to go completely dry over a fire. The cast iron won't melt or warp, but the patina can quickly turn to ash without the protective influence of the moisture.

Wiping down a camp Dutch oven with oil before storage. *CHRISTINE CONNERS*

- Avoid placing very hot cast iron in cool water. The resulting thermal shock may warp or crack the metal. Wait for your cookware to cool to the touch before immersing or pouring in wash water.
- Rub or spray a thin layer of food-grade oil over the entire surface of your cookware, including the legs and handles, both before using and after each cleaning. Doing so before cooking will further build the durability and effectiveness of the nonstick coating. And doing so after cleaning will protect the patina and prevent rust during storage. Using paper towels to spread the oil makes the job easier and less messy.
- Use a long-handled wooden or silicone spoon for mixing and stirring in your Dutch oven. Occasional use of metal spoons is acceptable, but avoid sustained use of metal utensils, which can wear the patina over time.

STEP-BY-STEP LARGE-GROUP COOKING TUTORIAL

This section takes the new outdoor chef step by step through Okefenokee Cheese Grits, an easy and great-tasting breakfast recipe for a large group of 16 to 18 people. Even Scouts not normally fond of grits will love this. The cheese seals the deal. Serve with optional sliced melon, a side of meat, and juice, and daybreak will find your crew livin' large.

Follow this tutorial from start to finish. The recipe is easy and enjoyable and takes only about half an hour to prepare. Afterward, you'll be ready to jump into any of the other terrific recipes that await in the following pages.

Okefenokee Cheese Grits

First, gather the ingredients you'll need from home or from the grocery store:

1 teaspoon salt

3 cups unflavored quick grits, such as Quaker brand

½ cup (1 standard stick) butter

1 pound (4 cups) grated cheddar cheese

Once at camp, you'll also need 3 quarts (12 cups) of water

Now is also the time to gather your cooking equipment, if you haven't already done so:

Sturdy cook stove with fuel and lighter

Large cook pot (about 6-quart capacity or larger)

Long-handled wooden spoon

Long-handled serving ladle

Serving bowls, spoons, and napkins or paper towels

Wash and rinse basins, sponge, soap, and drying towel

Hand sanitizer

Pack all the gear for the road; but before leaving home, make sure that the cheese and butter are tightly sealed in a container or ziplock bag then placed on ice in a good-quality cooler until they are ready to be used at camp.

Once at camp, place the camp stove on a sturdy surface. Ensure that the stove's fuel reservoir is full and tightly sealed (if using liquid fuel) or securely connected to a cylinder (if using propane). Be safe. Cook well away from combustibles such as dry grass, trees, or wooden structures. Notify the Scouts who aren't assisting in the kitchen to stay clear of the cooking area while the stove is in operation.

Thoroughly wash your hands before beginning to cook.

Light the stove and carefully place the cook pot, filled with 3 quarts of water, onto the burner. Ensure that the pot and stove are stable.

Turn the burner to a high setting. Add salt to the pot and bring the water to a boil.

Reduce heat to medium (turn the control handle or valve about halfway from high to off). Add quick grits and cook for about 5 minutes, stirring frequently with the long-handled spoon. When stirring, be sure the spoon reaches to the bottom of the pot. Otherwise, the grits can scorch and burn.

Turn the stove off then add butter and cheese, fully blending them into the grits with the wooden spoon.

Remove the pot from the burner, and place it on a heat-resistant surface. Double-check the stove to be sure that the flame is extinguished. Allow the grits to cool for about 5 more minutes.

Using the ladle, serve the grits to your happy crowd.

Enjoy your meal, then place any leftovers in a food-safe container on ice in a cooler. Scrape as much of the food from the pot as possible when doing this.

Okefenokee Cheese Grits. TIM CONNERS

If any of the grits have scorched or strongly adhere to the pot, pour a couple of inches of water into the pot, splash over the inside walls of the pot, and let sit for a few minutes to allow the food to loosen.

An initial rinse using a small amount of water should remove much of the food residue. The pot can then be washed in a tub of warm, sudsy water. Finish with a rinse in a separate basin of clean water then dry. Do the same with the wooden spoon and ladle.

Congratulations! You've prepared your first outdoor recipe for a large group.

The recipe for ***Okefenokee Cheese Grits*** comes from Scott Simerly, Scoutmaster of Troop 204 in Apex, North Carolina.

Dutch Oven Anytime

"This recipe is great for breakfast, but it's equally good for lunch, dinner, or a snack at 1 a.m."

2 pounds ground sausage or beef

2 onions, chopped

1 (32-ounce) bag frozen Tater Tots

1 dozen eggs

8 ounces (2 cups) grated cheese (your choice)

Salt and ground black pepper to taste

Option: Serve with salsa, sour cream, and tortillas to make burritos.

PREPARATION AT CAMP:

1. Over 32 coals, brown the meat in the Dutch oven and carefully drain excess grease.
2. Add chopped onion and cook until they become translucent.
3. Evenly lay Tater Tots over top of browned meat-onion mixture.
4. Beat eggs in a large bowl then pour over Tater Tots.
5. Spread grated cheese over eggs.
6. Bake for about 30 minutes, using 21 coals on the lid and 11 briquettes under the oven, until cheese is a gooey mess. Refresh coals as required.
7. Add salt and black pepper to taste.

REQUIRED EQUIPMENT:

14-inch camp Dutch oven
Large mixing bowl

Glenn Larsen, Pocatello, Idaho
Assistant Scoutmaster
Troop 395, Grand Teton Council

A spectacular lakeside campsite for the troop.

SCOTT H. SIMERLY SR.

Servings: 10–12
Preparation Time: 1¼ hours
Challenge Level: Easy

Caramel French Toast

2 cups firmly packed brown sugar

1 cup (2 standard sticks) butter

2 tablespoons light corn syrup

1 dozen eggs

2½ cups milk

1½ teaspoons vanilla extract

¼ teaspoon salt

1 (about 1 pound) loaf French bread, cut into ½-inch-thick slices

"This is one of the recipes I've collected during my forty-plus years with Troop 31. We don't have any fancy names for our recipes. We just try them, and if we like them, we put them in our file."

PREPARATION AT CAMP:

1. In Dutch oven over 32 coals, combine sugar, butter, and corn syrup. Stir until sugar and butter are dissolved and thicken into caramel.
2. Remove oven from coals.
3. Combine eggs, milk, vanilla, and salt in a large bowl and whisk thoroughly.
4. Dip each piece of bread in egg mixture, covering completely, and layer on top of hot caramel, creating a base.
5. Place a second layer of dipped bread on top of the first layer, using up the bread pieces.
6. Pour any remaining egg mixture over bread slices.
7. Bake for about 45 minutes, using 21 coals on the lid and 11 briquettes under the oven, until top of bread is lightly browned. Refresh coals as required.

REQUIRED EQUIPMENT:

14-inch camp Dutch oven
Large mixing bowl

Delano LaGow, Oswego, Illinois
Committee Member
Troop 31, Three Fires Council

Servings: 10–12
Preparation Time: 1½ hours
Challenge Level: Easy

Cup O' Breakfast

6 cups frozen potatoes O'Brien, thawed

16 slices precooked bacon

2 dozen eggs

Salt and ground black pepper to taste

PREPARATION AT CAMP:

1. In well-greased muffin pans, place ¼ cup potatoes in bottom of each cup.
2. Cut each bacon slice into 3 equal pieces and place 2 pieces into each cup on top of the potatoes.
3. Crack 1 egg per muffin cup, pouring over bacon.
4. Loosely cover the tins with aluminum foil and cook over low flame on campfire grate or on top of hot logs.
5. Baking takes about 15 minutes, but lift foil periodically to check eggs. When the egg whites are firm, the dish is ready.
6. Remove pans from fire and allow to cool for a couple of minutes.
7. With a knife or fork, gently release egg muffins from tins. They hold together well and make for easy finger food.
8. Season with salt and black pepper to taste.

REQUIRED EQUIPMENT:

2 (12-count) muffin pans (because of potential for high heat, don't use nonstick cookware)
Aluminum foil

Michael Berry, Oakley, California
Den Leader
Pack 298, Mount Diablo Silverado Council

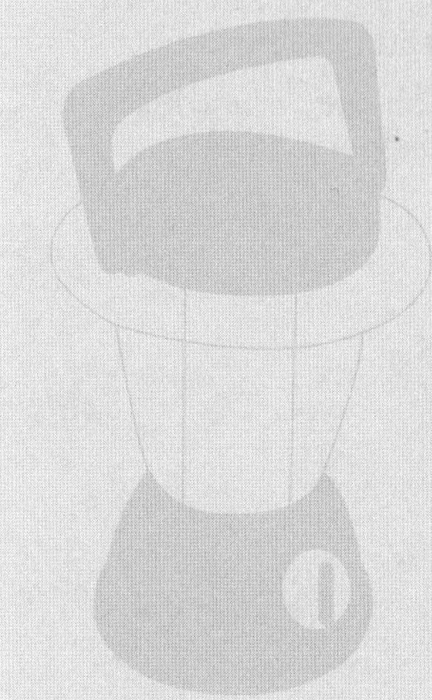

Servings: 12
Preparation Time: ½ hour
Challenge Level: Moderate

Great Rivers Corned Beef Hash

1 dozen eggs

6 tablespoons vegetable oil

2 onions, finely chopped

2 bell peppers, finely chopped

2 (12-ounce) cans corned beef

2 (30-ounce) bags frozen shredded hash brown potatoes, thawed

Salt and ground black pepper to taste

"I got the idea for this recipe while having breakfast in a famous 'hash house' in Chicago years ago. While eating, I thought, 'Man, we could do this on a campout sometime.' Most of the boys had never heard of corned beef. But they quickly forgot the 'corn' part, and the 'beef' carried the day. It became a popular dish with the patrols."

PREPARATION AT CAMP:

1. Fry eggs, over-easy or sunny-side-up, in a large, well-oiled skillet.
2. Set eggs aside and cover to help retain heat.
3. Heat vegetable oil in the skillet.
4. Sauté onions and bell pepper until onions are translucent.
5. Crumble corned beef into the skillet then add potatoes and salt and black pepper to taste. Occasionally stir mixture until potatoes are warmed through.
6. Top each serving with a fried egg.

REQUIRED EQUIPMENT:

Large frying pan

Richard Parkhurst, Sedalia, Missouri
Council Member
Great Rivers Council

Servings: 12
Preparation Time: ¾ hour
Challenge Level: Easy

Eggs á la Cheek

"At a Scouter Show-n-Do back in 1975, I combined two of my favorite Dutch oven recipes, and the rest is history. I used my own last name as a joke, and it stuck. I've cooked this recipe in Junior Leader Training, Woodbadge, and district and council training events. It even won a Roundtable cook-off years ago."

2 pounds sliced bacon, each slice cut into 1-inch pieces

2 (28-ounce) bags Ore-Ida O'Brien frozen hash browns, thawed

½ teaspoon salt

½ teaspoon ground black pepper

16 eggs

½ cup water

8 ounces (2 cups) shredded cheese (your choice)

Option: Substitute pork sausage for bacon or use no meat at all.

PREPARATION AT CAMP:

1. Heat Dutch oven over 32 coals and fry the bacon.
2. Add hash brown mixture, salt, and black pepper then stir occasionally until the potatoes are heated through.
3. Spread hash browns evenly over bottom of oven and use a large spoon to make depressions in the surface of the potatoes, one for each of the eggs.
4. Crack eggs into the depressions.
5. Pour water around the edges of the Dutch oven (not on the eggs).
6. Cover and move 21 coals from under the oven to the lid. Bake for 5 to 10 minutes, until the eggs are cooked.
7. Remove lid, sprinkle cheese over top of eggs and hash browns, and replace lid until cheese melts, about 5 additional minutes.

REQUIRED EQUIPMENT:

14-inch camp Dutch oven

Bob Cheek, Fort Atkinson, Wisconsin
Eagle Scout and Camp Director
Camp Indian Trails, Glacier's Edge Council

Servings: 14–16
Preparation Time: 1¼ hours
Challenge Level: Easy

Apple Sausage French Toast

2 pounds ground pork sausage

6 medium Granny Smith apples, cored, peeled, and cut into ½-inch-thick slices

12 eggs

1½ cups milk

1 cup maple syrup

1 teaspoon nutmeg

1 (about 1-pound) loaf French bread, cup into ½-inch thick slices

PREPARATION AT CAMP:

1. In Dutch oven heated over 32 coals, brown sausage until meat is no longer pink.
2. Remove sausage and set aside. Drain excess grease.
3. Add sliced apples to the hot oven then cover and cook for 3 to 5 minutes, until tender. Remove apples and set aside.
4. In a large bowl, whisk eggs, milk, syrup, and nutmeg until combined.
5. Dip about half of the bread slices in the egg mixture, fully coating each, then arrange on the bottom of the oven.
6. Evenly cover bread at the bottom of the oven with the browned sausage, followed by the cooked apples, and finally with the remaining bread slices, also thoroughly dipped in the egg mix.
7. Pour any remaining egg mixture over the top.
8. Bake for about 45 minutes, using 21 coals on the lid and 11 briquettes under the oven, until the bread is lightly browned. Refresh coals as required.

REQUIRED EQUIPMENT:

14-inch camp Dutch oven
Large mixing bowl

Delano LaGow, Oswego, Illinois
Committee Member
Troop 31, Three Fires Council

Servings: 14–16
Preparation Time: 1½ hours
Challenge Level: Moderate

Greeting the day with perfect pancakes. CHRISTINE CONNER

Rib-Stickin' Biscuits and Gravy

"I've made this recipe on many camping trips. Make sure you don't have any lunch plans for the day, because you may not have the appetite for it. This stuff really sticks to your ribs."

2 (12-ounce, 8-count) packages refrigerated buttermilk biscuits

1 pound ground sausage (medium-spicy or sage-flavored)

¼ cup all-purpose flour

4 cups milk

1½ teaspoons ground white pepper

1 teaspoon ground black pepper

¼ teaspoon salt

PREPARATION AT CAMP:

1. Place biscuits side by side in preheated Dutch oven with 21 coals on the lid and 11 briquettes under the oven.
2. Bake for about 15 minutes, until the biscuits become a golden brown.
3. While biscuits bake, brown sausage in a large skillet.
4. Remove sausage from skillet, leaving grease in the pan.
5. Mix flour in the skillet until dissolved.
6. Stir milk into the flour a little at a time.
7. Add white and black pepper and salt then stir.
8. Return sausage to the skillet.
9. Simmer while stirring until gravy thickens and begins to bubble.
10. Serve gravy over opened biscuits.

REQUIRED EQUIPMENT:

14-inch camp Dutch oven
Large frying pan

Jason Cagle, Jacksonville, Florida
Assistant Scoutmaster
Troop 169, North Florida Council

Servings: 16
Preparation Time: 1 hour
Challenge Level: Moderate

Geezer Patrol Stuffed French Toast

3 (about 1-pound) loaves French bread, sliced 1 to 1½ inches thick

2 (8-ounce) packages cream cheese, softened

1 (32-ounce) jar seedless jam (your favorite)

4 cups cornflakes

2 dozen eggs, beaten

1 cup milk

1 tablespoon almond extract

1 teaspoon vanilla extract

½ cup (1 standard stick) butter

Maple or pancake syrup to taste

"In our troop, the adults form their own 'patrol' on campouts, usually dining separately from the youth. Having grown tired of plain French toast, the 'Geezer Patrol' came up with the following."

PREPARATION AT CAMP:

1. Make a pocket in the side of each slice of bread using a sharp paring knife.
2. Knead the cream cheese together with the jam in a gallon-size ziplock bag.
3. Cut a small corner from the ziplock bag. Holding the bread in one hand, squeeze a small amount of cream cheese–jam blend into the pocket in each slice of bread. Carefully meter the jam blend to be sure there is enough for all slices.
4. Crush cornflakes in a large bowl and set aside.
5. In a second large bowl, beat together the eggs, milk, and extracts.
6. Melt butter in a large skillet over medium heat.
7. Dip each slice of French toast in the egg mixture to coat, then press each into the cornflakes, lightly coating the bread on both sides with the cereal.
8. Cook each slice in the skillet on both sides until golden brown.
9. Serve, topping with maple or pancake syrup to taste.

REQUIRED EQUIPMENT:

Large frying pan
2 large mixing bowls
Gallon-size heavy-duty ziplock bag

John Malachowski, Stewartstown, Pennsylvania
Scoutmaster
Troop 27, New Birth of Freedom Council

Servings: 18–20
Preparation Time: ¾ hour
Challenge Level: Moderate

Croque Madame

"Here's one way to spice up the name for ham and cheese: call it 'croque madame,' which, as a French phrase, refers to the sandwich, but translated literally, means 'lady undertaker'—not quite as appealing. A colleague of mine who was raised in Belgium suggested Croque Madame as traditional fare for my pack. Our recipe was a finalist in the international-themed Cubmaster Cook-Off at the Coastal Empire Council's 100th Anniversary Scout Expo. We were beaten out for the coveted Silver Spatula Award by another recipe of ours, a Pumpkin Torte."

Option: The adults usually enjoy their croque madame per the recipe. However, many of the Cub Scouts request theirs "sans oeuf," without the egg.

PREPARATION AT CAMP:

1. Butter both sides of each slice of bread using about ¼ tablespoon per slice.
2. Place a slice of cheese and a slice of ham between 2 slices of bread to make a sandwich.
3. Grill each sandwich in a large frying pan.
4. Meanwhile, in a second large skillet, fry the eggs.
5. Place 1 egg on top of each grilled sandwich.
6. Serve warm, adding salt and black pepper to taste.

REQUIRED EQUIPMENT:

2 large frying pans

Jimmy Hancock, Savannah, Georgia
Eagle Scout and Cubmaster
Pack 11, Coastal Empire Council

Servings			
8	**16**	**24**	**Ingredients**
4 tbsp	8 tbsp	12 tbsp	butter, softened
16	32	48	slices bread, your choice but not thick-sliced
8	16	24	slices Swiss cheese
8	16	24	slices ham
8	16	24	eggs
			salt and ground black pepper to taste

Servings: 8–24
Preparation Time: ½ hour
Challenge Level: Easy

Breakfast Omelet Burrito Buffet

PREPARATION AT CAMP:

1. Place Mexicorn, cheese, black beans, and salsa toppings into separate serving bowls.
2. Whisk eggs with milk in a large mixing bowl.
3. Add oil or butter to warm skillet then pour in the egg mixture, scrambling until fully cooked. For very large crowds, the egg mixture may require preparation in more than one batch.
4. Divide eggs among the tortillas and have the Scouts and Scouters add their favorite toppings.
5. Add salt and black pepper to taste.
6. Fold like a burrito.

REQUIRED EQUIPMENT:

Large frying pan
Large mixing bowl

Harold Robinson, Quarryville, Pennsylvania
Assistant Scoutmaster
Troop 58, Pennsylvania Dutch Council

Servings			
8	**16**	**24**	**Ingredients**
1	2	3	11-ounce cans Mexicorn
4 ounces	8 ounces	12 ounces	shredded cheese (your choice)
1	2	3	15-ounce cans seasoned black beans, drained
1	2	3	16-ounce jars mild chunky salsa
1 dozen	2 dozen	3 dozen	eggs
1	2	3	cups milk
2	4	6	tablespoon oil or butter
8	16	24	large flour tortillas
			salt and ground black pepper to taste

Servings: 8–24
Preparation Time: ½ hour
Challenge Level: Easy

German Apple Pancakes

"This dish is great on a cold campout."

PREPARATION AT CAMP:

1. Pour water in skillet, just enough to cover the bottom.
2. Add apples, brown sugar, apricot jelly, and cinnamon to the frying pan.
3. Bring skillet to a simmer until the water boils off and the sugar begins to slightly caramelize. It may be necessary to drain some of the water to hasten the process. Remove skillet from heat.
4. Mix flour, milk, eggs, sugar, baking soda, and butter in a large bowl until smooth.
5. Add caramelized apples and any optional ingredients to the bowl with the flour mix. Stir well.
6. Scrape skillet clean with spatula to reuse it for cooking pancakes.
7. Prepare individual pancakes in skillet as with a traditional recipe, using butter to grease pan. Flip when one side begins to bubble then quickly finish the opposite side to prevent burning.
8. Serve with syrup.

REQUIRED EQUIPMENT:

Large frying pan
Large mixing bowl

Servings: 8–24
Preparation Time: ¾ hour
Challenge Level: Moderate

Michael Kaiserauer, Berlin, Germany
Eagle Scout and Scoutmaster
Troop 895, Transatlantic Council

Servings			
8	**16**	**24**	**Ingredients**
			water, just enough to cover bottom of skillet
2	4	6	large Granny Smith apples, cored, peeled, and chopped
2 tbsp	4 tbsp	6 tbsp	brown sugar
2 tbsp	4 tbsp	6 tbsp	apricot jelly
½ tbsp	1 tbsp	1½ tbsp	ground cinnamon
2 cups	4 cups	6 cups	all-purpose flour
1¾ cups	3½ cups	5¼ cups	milk
2	4	6	eggs
¼ cup	½ cup	¾ cup	granulated sugar
2 tbsp	4 tbsp	6 tbsp	baking soda
2 tbsp	4 tbsp	6 tbsp	butter, softened, plus additional to fry
			syrup (your favorite) optional: raisins or chocolate chips

Campfire Eggs Benedict

"I live in Germany, so it was a treat for the Scouts and Scouters in our troop in Munich to be introduced to an all-American classic. This recipe proves that America has great cuisine, even at camp. It sounds difficult, but when adapted to a campfire, as done here with fried eggs and the use of whole eggs in the hollandaise sauce, it isn't difficult. It's about as good as any you'll find in restaurants."

Option: Recipe can also be eaten sandwich-style by placing a second half of toasted muffin on top.

PREPARATION AT CAMP:

1. In a dry skillet over an open fire, toast the English muffin halves. Don't let the muffins burn.
2. While the muffins are being prepared, melt butter in a medium-size pot.
3. Remove pot from the flame and add lemon juice and eggs specified for the hollandaise sauce.
4. Place pot back over medium flame, stirring constantly until thick. Don't allow the mixture to curdle.
5. Add sour cream, stir, then heat for about a minute, being careful not to boil (which would cause the sauce to separate).
6. Add salt and black pepper to taste and set hollandaise sauce aside.
7. In the same skillet used to toast the bread, use a bit of butter to grease skillet and fry ham on both sides. Set ham aside.
8. Fry eggs, one for each muffin, either sunny-side-up or over-easy.
9. Salt and pepper the eggs to taste.
10. On each serving plate, place half of a toasted muffin, cut-side up.

Servings: 8–24
Preparation Time: 1 hour
Challenge Level: Moderate

11. Top with one slice of fried ham and one fried egg each.
12. Finish by pouring a bit of hollandaise sauce on each, being careful to reserve enough for each serving.

REQUIRED EQUIPMENT:

Large frying pan
Medium-size cook pot

Charles Bostick, Munich, Germany
Eagle Scout and Assistant Scoutmaster
Troop 21, Transatlantic Council

Servings			
8	**16**	**24**	**Ingredients**
4	8	12	English muffins, halved
4 tablespoons	8 tablespoons	12 tablespoons	butter, plus extra for greasing the skillet
2 tablespoons	4 tablespoons	6 tablespoons	lemon juice, fresh squeezed
2	4	6	eggs (for hollandaise sauce)
1 cup	2 cups	3 cups	sour cream
			salt and ground black pepper to taste
8	16	24	slices ham, thick sliced
8	16	24	eggs (for muffin)

Eggs, sunny-side-up with fresh cracked pepper.
CHRISTINE CONNERS

Trapper Trails Scrambled Eggs

"Sooooooo easy. Sooooooo good."

PREPARATION AT CAMP:

1. Whisk eggs and milk together in a large bowl. For larger number of servings, the eggs may need to be prepared in batches.
2. Warm butter in a large skillet over low heat. Coat the bottom of the skillet with butter once it melts.
3. Pour egg mixture into pan and add cubes of cream cheese. Add salt, black pepper, and optional garlic and onions at this time.
4. Stir continually until eggs are finished cooking.

REQUIRED EQUIPMENT:

Large frying pan
Large bowl

Sandra Dopp, Richmond, Utah
Roundtable Staff
Trapper Trails Council

Servings			
10	**20**	**30**	**Ingredients**
2 dozen	4 dozen	6 dozen	eggs
1 cup	2 cups	3 cups	milk
2 tablespoons	4 tablespoons	6 tablespoons	butter
1	2	3	8-ounce packages cream cheese, cubed
			salt and ground black pepper to taste
			optional: minced garlic and diced green onions to taste

Servings: 10–30
Preparation Time: ¼ hour
Challenge Level: Easy

Italian Bear Bait with Pasta

"My son and I created this recipe together because he loves pasta and he wanted to have tasty food on his campouts."

2 pounds lean ground beef

1 medium onion, diced

1 medium red or green bell pepper, diced

1 teaspoon minced garlic

1 teaspoon onion powder

1 teaspoon dried Italian seasoning

½ teaspoon salt

½ teaspoon crushed red pepper

1 teaspoon ground cumin

2 (14½-ounce) cans diced tomatoes with basil, garlic, and oregano

1 (28-ounce) can Italian-style chunky crushed tomatoes

1 (1-pound) box rotini or bow-tie pasta

½ cup grated Parmesan cheese

PREPARATION AT CAMP:

1. In a large frying pan, brown ground beef over medium flame.
2. Add diced onions, bell peppers, and minced garlic, stirring constantly.
3. Add all the spices along with the diced and crushed tomatoes. Stir well.
4. Bring to a simmer and cook for 25 minutes.
5. Meanwhile, cook pasta in medium-size pot per directions on box, then drain.
6. Serve meat sauce over pasta or mix meat sauce and pasta together.
7. Top with grated Parmesan cheese and serve.

REQUIRED EQUIPMENT:

Medium-size cook pot
Large frying pan

Jenny George, Ivyland, Pennsylvania
Committee Member
Troop 400, Bucks County Council

Servings: 10–12
Preparation Time: ¾ hour
Challenge Level: Easy

Quivira Chicken Potpie

1 (22-ounce) package Tyson Grilled & Ready chicken breasts, thawed and cut into small cubes

1 (30-ounce) bag frozen shredded hash browns, thawed

1 (16-ounce) bag frozen mixed vegetables (carrots, peas, and green beans), thawed

1 (1-ounce) package Lipton dry onion soup mix

1 (12-ounce) can evaporated milk

1 (10¾-ounce) can condensed cream of mushroom soup

1 (10¾-ounce) can condensed cream of chicken soup

2 (8-ounce, 8-count) containers refrigerated crescent rolls

PREPARATION AT CAMP:

1. Combine all ingredients except crescent rolls in Dutch oven. Stir thoroughly.
2. Layer unrolled crescent roll dough over top of ingredients like a pinwheel, with the points of the long ends of each piece meeting at the center.
3. Bake for about 35 minutes, using 21 coals on the lid and 11 briquettes under the oven, until dough is a golden brown.

REQUIRED EQUIPMENT:

14-inch camp Dutch oven

Ray Willems, Hutchinson, Kansas
Scoutmaster
Troop 306, Quivira Council

Dutch oven chicken potpie. *CHRISTINE CONNERS*

Servings: 10–12
Preparation Time: 1 hour
Challenge Level: Easy

Katastrophe Kabobs (Disaster-Averted Version)

"How difficult could it be to spear some veggies and chunks of meat and throw them on the grill? The first time I prepared this, it didn't take long for significant flames to be noticeable from the grill. After the flames died down, I lifted the lid to discover to my dismay that most of the meat and vegetables were lying in the coals. The flames had been from the wooden skewers burning because I had not first soaked them in water. That was the first and last time I made that mistake."

1 (10-ounce) bottle soy sauce

1 (16-ounce) bottle Italian salad dressing

1 cup of honey

1 (20-ounce) can pineapple chunks, juice reserved

MIX AND MATCH YOUR FAVORITES:

2 pounds boneless chicken breasts, sirloin, or shrimp

2 bell peppers, cored and cut into 1-inch squares

2 zucchinis, halved lengthwise and cut into ½-inch-thick half-rounds

2 yellow squash, halved lengthwise and cut into ½-inch-thick half-rounds

8 ounces whole fresh mushrooms

1 large red or brown onion, peeled and cut into 1-inch thick wedges

1 pint cherry tomatoes

PREPARATION AT CAMP:

1. Combine soy sauce, Italian dressing, and honey in a medium-size bowl.
2. Add juice from pineapple can to the bowl.
3. Stir, then divide marinade between two heavy-duty 1-gallon-size ziplock bags.
4. If using chicken or sirloin, cut meat into 1-inch cubes.
5. Place meat or shrimp into one of the ziplock bags.
6. Place pineapple and vegetables into other ziplock bag.
7. Seal both bags tightly and shake the bags so that the contents are fully coated with marinade.
8. Place bags on ice in a cooler to marinate for at least 2 hours.
9. Thread pineapple, meat, and vegetables onto 24 12-inch-long skewers, leaving a small gap in between items for more even cooking. Skewer squash and zucchini through their sides.
10. Cook kabobs on a grill over medium heat until meat is thoroughly cooked through.

REQUIRED EQUIPMENT:

Medium-size mixing bowl
2 (1-gallon-size) heavy-duty ziplock bags
24 (12-inch) long skewers (presoak wooden skewers in water)

Mary Young, Sunset, Louisiana
Committee Member
Troop 143, Evangeline Area Council

Servings: 12
Preparation Time: 3 hours (including 2 hours for marinating)
Challenge Level: Moderate

Ken's Mac & Cheese

2 pounds elbow macaroni pasta

⅓ cup cornstarch

2 teaspoons powdered mustard

1 teaspoon ground black pepper

Ground cayenne pepper to taste (optional)

1 quart water

2 (12-ounce) cans evaporated milk

1 pound sharp cheddar cheese, cubed

1 pound regular cheddar, Gruyère, or Jack cheese, cubed

½ (16-ounce) box Ritz crackers

Option: For a healthier option, use reduced-fat evaporated milk and cheeses.

PREPARATION AT CAMP:

1. Fill a large pot two-thirds full with water and bring to a boil.
2. Add macaroni and cook until just tender, typically 8 to 10 minutes.
3. Meanwhile, place cornstarch, powdered mustard, black pepper, and optional cayenne powder in a medium-size cook pot and blend with 1 quart of water.
4. Add evaporated milk and cheese cubes to the cornstarch mixture and bring to a low boil.
5. Simmer the cheese sauce for about 2 minutes while stirring constantly, until the cheese is entirely melted and the sauce thickens.
6. Once the pasta is finished cooking, drain thoroughly, then add the prepared cheese sauce to the pasta. Gently stir.
7. Distribute several Ritz crackers per serving to be crushed as a topping.

REQUIRED EQUIPMENT:

Large cook pot
Medium-size cook pot

Ken Harbison, Rochester, New York
Former Boy Scout and Master Tester for *The Scout's Outdoor Cookbook*
Washington Trail Council

Servings: 14–16
Preparation Time: ½ hour
Challenge Level: Easy

Spicy Chicken Wrapsidy

"This is a great main course, starter, or even a side. It's easy to make, and the cleanup is quick. The recipe can be spicy, so have the fire bucket ready."

1 (8-ounce) package cream cheese

1 (6-ounce) container plain yogurt

1 (8-ounce) jar spicy hot salsa

3 tablespoons chopped fresh cilantro leaves

1 (2¼-ounce) can sliced black olives

1 red onion, finely diced

2 small red chile peppers, finely diced

Juice from a lime

8 chicken breast fillets

2 tablespoons olive oil

2 tablespoons chile pepper powder

16 large soft tortillas

PREPARATION AT CAMP:

1. In a medium-size bowl, mix together cream cheese, yogurt, salsa, cilantro, black olives, onion, chile peppers, and about half of the lime juice.
2. Cut the chicken breast fillets into long strips about ¾ inch in width.
3. Preheat frying pan with olive oil and fry the chicken strips with chile powder and remaining lime juice until chicken is browned and cooked through.
4. Remove from heat and place chicken on paper towels to drain excess oil.
5. Spread 1 heaping tablespoon of salsa-cheese mix on each tortilla.
6. Place 2 to 3 chicken strips on the mix and roll into a tight wrap. Allow to cool if necessary.
7. Cut each wrap into 4 equal pieces.

REQUIRED EQUIPMENT:

Large frying pan
Medium-size mixing bowl

Michael Kaiserauer, Berlin, Germany
Eagle Scout and Scoutmaster
Troop 895, Transatlantic Council

Servings: 16
Preparation Time: ¾ hour
Challenge Level: Easy

Mondo Dogs

2 pounds lean ground beef

1 small yellow onion, diced (or 2 teaspoons onion powder)

2 teaspoons garlic powder

1 tablespoon oregano

½ teaspoon salt

3 tablespoons barbecue sauce

1 tablespoon Worcestershire sauce

8 cheddar bratwursts

16 bacon strips

8 hoagie rolls

Condiments: catsup, mustard, mayonnaise, pickle relish

"The boys scoffed at the idea of a 'burger-dog,' so the adults made them for lunch one day, ostensibly for the leaders only. Knowing full well we'd end up sharing them, we made sure to have enough to go around as 'samples.' Word soon spread that there were hot dogs—wrapped in cheese, wrapped in hamburger, wrapped in bacon—sitting on the fire. The boys dropped the PB&Js they had made for themselves and gathered round the flames. By the time the burger-dogs were finished cooking, I felt like the Pied Piper, explaining to my troops-in-tow that the meal need not be fancy or difficult to be fun and fantastic. This was the beginning of a legend in our troop: the amazing Mondo Dog."

PREPARATION AT CAMP:

1. Blend ground beef and onion in medium-size mixing bowl.
2. Add garlic powder, oregano, salt, barbecue sauce, and Worcestershire sauce to beef mixture and blend well.
3. Form 8 oval patties from the beef mixture. The patties should be about 1 inch longer than the brats and wide enough to wrap them.
4. Fully wrap each of the bratwursts in a ground beef patty.
5. Wrap 1 piece of bacon around the whole burger-dog in one direction diagonally then wrap a second piece of bacon around the dog in the opposite direction diagonally. The bacon helps hold the burger-dog together and should cover the outside of the dog in a crisscross pattern. Secure the bacon strips in place with toothpicks.
6. On the grill or over the fire, cook for about 20 to 25 minutes, rotating occasionally and controlling flare-ups. The outsides should be covered in crispy bacon once they are ready, but use a food thermometer to be sure bratwurst is fully cooked to 165°F.
7. Serve on hoagie rolls with your favorite condiments.

TIP: These are extremely filling, and each dog is divided in half in this recipe to produce reasonable serving sizes.

Servings: 16 (2 servings per dog)
Preparation Time: 1 hour
Challenge Level: Moderate

REQUIRED EQUIPMENT:

Medium-size mixing bowl
Toothpicks

Shawn Collins, Aiken, South Carolina
Assistant Scoutmaster
Troop 68, Central New Jersey Council

Camp Boxwell's Taco-in-a-Bowl

"This recipe took first place in the Dutch oven cook-off at Camp Boxwell Winter Camp in 2009."

2 pounds lean ground beef

2 small onions, diced

2 (11-ounce) cans Mexicorn

2 (15-ounce) cans light red kidney beans, drained

2 (15-ounce) cans black beans, drained

2 (10-ounce) cans Ro*Tel diced tomatoes

2 (15-ounce) cans tomato sauce

2 (1½-ounce) packets taco seasoning

3 large Roma tomatoes, cubed

1 head iceberg lettuce, shredded

8 ounces (2 cups) shredded cheddar cheese

1 (16-ounce) container sour cream

2 (16-ounce) jars salsa

2 (10½-ounce) bags corn chips

PREPARATION AT CAMP:

1. In a very large skillet, brown ground beef with the diced onions.
2. Add to this the Mexicorn, kidney beans, black beans, Ro*Tel tomatoes, tomato sauce, and taco seasoning.
3. Thoroughly warm the meat-bean mixture over low heat, stirring occasionally.
4. Place tomatoes, lettuce, shredded cheese, sour cream, and salsa in individual serving bowls.
5. Have Scouts and Scouters place corn chips in the bottoms of their bowls.
6. Cover corn chips with meat-bean mixture, then add tomatoes and the rest of the toppings as desired.

REQUIRED EQUIPMENT:

Large frying pan

Allen King, Madison, Alabama
Eagle Scout
Venture Crew 7, Greater Alabama Council

Servings: 20–22
Preparation Time: ½ hours
Challenge Level: Easy

Prairielands Pizza Stew

2 pounds rotini noodles

2 pounds lean ground beef

2 onions, chopped

2 green bell peppers, chopped

4 (14-ounce) jars pizza sauce

1 (6-ounce) package sliced pepperoni

1 (8-ounce) can mushrooms, drained

1 teaspoon garlic powder

Optional "toppings": olives, ham, pineapple, tomatoes, banana peppers

2 pounds (8 cups) shredded mozzarella cheese

"The kids love this recipe. As with traditional pizza, the ingredients can be adjusted to your group's preferences. We delete items if someone doesn't like them and add favorites at request."

PREPARATION AT CAMP:

1. Boil noodles until tender in large cook pot. Drain.
2. While noodles cook, brown ground beef in medium-size skillet over medium heat.
3. Once meat is brown, set aside, then sauté onions and peppers in oil left from cooking the meat.
4. Add to the noodles the browned ground beef, sautéed onions and peppers, pizza sauce, pepperoni, mushrooms, and garlic powder, along with any optional "toppings."
5. Heat until warm over medium flame.
6. Remove from heat then stir in the cheese, saving some to sprinkle on top when serving.

REQUIRED EQUIPMENT:

Large cook pot
Medium-size skillet

Herbert Hutnak Jr., Ashkum, Illinois
Scoutmaster
Troop 158, Prairielands Council

Venture Crew camp chefs come to the rescue.

SCOTT H. SIMERLY SR.

Servings: 20–22
Preparation Time: ¾ hour
Challenge Level: Easy

Walking Sloppy Joes

PREPARATION AT CAMP:

1. Brown beef with the onions in a large skillet.
2. Add tomato soup, ketchup, brown sugar, and seasoned salt.
3. Stir until heated through.
4. Serve over Fritos or on buns.

REQUIRED EQUIPMENT:

Large frying pan

Kimberly Barber, Byron Center, Michigan
Assistant Scoutmaster
Troop 250, Gerald R. Ford Council

Servings			
8	**16**	**24**	**Ingredients**
1 pound	2 pounds	3 pounds	lean ground beef
1	2	3	medium onions, chopped
1	2	3	10¾-ounce cans condensed tomato soup
½ cup	1 cup	1½ cups	ketchup
2 tablespoons	4 tablespoons	6 tablespoons	brown sugar
1 tablespoons	2 tablespoons	3 tablespoons	Lawry's Seasoned Salt
2	4	6	9¼-ounce bags Fritos corn chips or . . .
1	2	3	8-count packs hamburger buns (instead of Fritos)

Servings: 8–24
Preparation Time: ½ hour
Challenge Level: Easy

Fiesta-in-a-Flash Chicken Wraps

PREPARATION AT CAMP:

1. Divide chicken among tortillas, spreading a line of meat down the center of each.
2. Top chicken with cheese and salsa.
3. Wrap like burritos, tucking in the sides of the tortilla before rolling.
4. Use foil packs, placing several wrapped burritos into each, or lay burrito wraps side by side on a "tray" made from heavy-duty aluminum foil.
5. Heat over a low fire or on the grill over coals until cheese is melted and chicken is hot.
6. Top with lettuce, tomatoes, avocados, and sour cream, or eat as is.

REQUIRED EQUIPMENT:

Heavy-duty aluminum foil

Tina Knott, Somerset, Pennsylvania
Committee Chair
Troop 5152, Penn's Woods Council

Servings			
8	**16**	**24**	**Ingredients**
2	4	6	12½-ounce cans cooked chicken, drained
8	16	24	flour tortillas, burrito-style
½ pound	1 pound	1½ pounds	shredded pepper Jack cheese or Mexican-style
8 ounces	16 ounces	24 ounces	salsa (your favorite)
⅓ head	⅔ head	1 head	iceberg lettuce, shredded
2	4	6	tomatoes, diced
2	4	6	avocados, sliced into wedges
8 ounces	16 ounces	24 ounces	sour cream

Servings: 8–24
Preparation Time: ½ hour
Challenge Level: Easy

Pigs in Sleeping Bags

PREPARATION AT CAMP:

1. Place each hot dog on its own campfire roasting fork.
2. Cook dog until meat is just warmed through but before outside begins to char.
3. Carefully place hot dog into the pocket of a biscuit.
4. Wrap biscuit around hot dog. Stretch dough to cover most of the length of the dog, and pinch dough together at one end and up the side to form the "sleeping bag."
5. Place pig-in-a-sleeping-bag back onto fork, piercing through the dough "bag" to secure it.
6. Continue to cook over fire. The dogs are ready to serve with condiments once the biscuits become a golden brown, about 10 additional minutes.

REQUIRED EQUIPMENT:

Campfire roasting forks

Delano LaGow, Oswego, Illinois
Committee Member
Troop 31, Three Fires Council

Servings			
8	**16**	**24**	**Ingredients**
8	16	24	regular-size hot dogs
1	2	3	8-count containers jumbo refrigerated biscuits
			condiments (your favorites)

Servings: 8–24
Preparation Time: ½ hour
Challenge Level: Easy

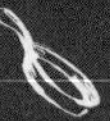

CB MELT (Cheese, Bacon, Mayo, Egg, Lettuce, and Tomato)

PREPARATION AT CAMP:

1. Toast bread in frying pan or over fire.
2. Cook bacon in frying pan until crisp.
3. Hard-fry the eggs in the bacon grease.
4. Lightly spread mayonnaise on one side of each slice of toast.
5. Place 2 slices bacon, 1 egg, 1 cheese slice, 1 lettuce leaf, and 2 tomato slices between 2 pieces of bread.

REQUIRED EQUIPMENT:

Large frying pan

Jason Cagle, Jacksonville, Florida
Assistant Scoutmaster
Troop 169, North Florida Council

Servings			
8	**16**	**24**	**Ingredients**
16	32	48	slices bread (your favorite)
16	32	48	slices bacon
8	16	24	large eggs
1	1	1	jar mayonnaise
8	16	24	slices cheese (Swiss, American, or provolone)
8	16	24	leaves romaine lettuce
16	32	48	slices tomato

Servings: 8–24
Preparation Time: ½ hour
Challenge Level: Moderate

Camp Shands Chicken Salad

"During my culinary days, I worked in a French-Italian bistro that made a salad similar to this recipe. The blend of the sweet and salty flavors really make it a hit."

PREPARATION AT CAMP:

1. Fill stockpot about halfway with water then add salt, olive oil, Worcestershire, and rosemary. Bring to a boil.
2. Add chicken breasts. Boil meat until cooked through.
3. Cool chicken breasts in ziplock bags buried in ice for about 15 minutes.
4. Dice chicken into ½-inch cubes.
5. In a large mixing bowl, blend cubed chicken, onion, celery, walnuts, and grapes with vinegar, mayonnaise, and black pepper until evenly mixed.
6. Serve over a leaf of romaine lettuce with optional butter crackers.

REQUIRED EQUIPMENT:

Medium-size cook pot
Large mixing bowl
Several gallon-size heavy-duty ziplock bags

Option: This recipe can also be prepared at home and refrigerated until needed at camp.

Jason Cagle, Jacksonville, Florida
Assistant Scoutmaster
Troop 169, North Florida Council

Servings: 8–24
Preparation Time: 1 hour
Challenge Level: Moderate

Servings			
8	**16**	**24**	**Ingredients**
1 tablespoon	1 tablespoon	1 tablespoon	salt
¼ cup	¼ cup	¼ cup	virgin olive oil
¼ cup	¼ cup	¼ cup	Worcestershire sauce
6 tablespoons	6 tablespoons	6 tablespoons	rosemary, fresh or dried
4	8	12	large boneless chicken breasts
½	1	1½	red onions, diced
5	10	15	stalks celery, diced
¼ cup	½ cup	¾ cup	chopped walnuts
½ cup	1 cup	1½ cups	halved red grapes
3 tablespoons	6 tablespoons	9 tablespoons	red wine vinegar
½ cup	1 cup	1½ cups	mayonnaise
4 teaspoons	8 teaspoons	4 tablespoons	ground black pepper
8	16	24	leaves romaine lettuce
			optional: butter crackers

Troop 854's Officially Banned Jamaican Chicken Burrito Recipe

ONION-PEPPER SAUCE:

6 Scotch bonnet or habañero chilies, cut in half, stemmed, and seeded

4 cups (about 10 ounces) chopped green onions

½ cup honey

½ cup cider vinegar

½ cup low-sodium soy sauce

4 teaspoons ground allspice

1 teaspoon ground cinnamon

1 teaspoon ground thyme

2 teaspoons salt

8 cloves garlic, crushed

4 pounds chicken thighs, skin removed (or 3 pounds boneless chicken)

24 flour tortillas

2 cups (8 ounces) shredded mild cheddar cheese

1 (16-ounce) container sour cream

½ head cabbage, shredded

1 bunch cilantro, washed and chopped

Servings: 24
Preparation Time: 6½ hours (see Tip for more information)
Challenge Level: Moderate

"This dish made its debut at the West Point Scoutmaster's Camporee at the United States Military Academy in New York. Our troop had been to this Camporee three times before, and each time never placed in the cooking competition. We really wanted to change that with this recipe. We knew we had the winner when several Cadets came back for seconds, then thirds, finally sending their hungry friends from competing troops to try the dish. Since then, this recipe has taken first place at many cooking competitions. Due to its infallible winning ability, it's been officially banned from the District Camporee."

PREPARATION AT HOME:

1. Prepare onion-pepper sauce by combining chilies, chopped green onions, honey, vinegar, soy sauce, allspice, cinnamon, thyme, salt, and garlic in a blender. Puree until smooth.
2. Store sauce in a heavy-duty ziplock bag or sealable bowl. Keep chilled until ready to use at camp.

PREPARATION AT CAMP:

1. Place chicken in greased Dutch oven.
2. Pour most of onion-pepper sauce over top of chicken and gently stir to coat. Reserve a small amount of onion-pepper sauce for the final step.
3. Bake for about 6 hours, using 9 coals on the lid and 4 briquettes under the oven, until the chicken is "falling off the bone." Refresh coals as needed.
4. Once chicken is ready, remove meat from bones, shredding with a pair of forks.
5. Assemble burritos using tortillas, cheese, sour cream, cabbage, cilantro, and remaining onion-pepper sauce.

REQUIRED EQUIPMENT:

12-inch camp Dutch oven

Marc Robinson, Canton, Michigan
Eagle Scout and Assistant Scoutmaster
Troop 854, Great Lakes Council

"Add a few more coals and let's get this thing finished. I'm starving!" SCOTT H. SIMMERLY SR.

Option: For a more traditional flair, or to extend the base recipe to feed more people, 4 cups jasmine rice can be cooked as an additional burrito filling.

Caution: Scotch bonnet and habañero chilies are among the world's hottest. Use caution when preparing, and wear food preparation gloves to avoid getting the oils on your skin or in your eyes.

TIP:
Provided that the chicken is put over the coals very early in the day and tended to throughout the morning, this dish makes for a great lunch recipe because final preparation is quick and easy.

Nundawaga Steak Cobbler

- ½ cup all-purpose flour
- 1 teaspoon salt
- ½ teaspoon ground black pepper
- 2 pounds beef, top or bottom round, cut into ½-inch chunks
- 4 tablespoons vegetable oil
- 2 medium onions, peeled and cut into 1-inch-thick wedges
- 8 ounces sliced fresh mushrooms
- 1 (12-ounce) package frozen mixed vegetables (carrots, green beans, corn, peas), thawed
- 1 cup beef broth
- ½ teaspoon garlic powder
- ½ teaspoon ground cayenne pepper
- 1 teaspoon browning and seasoning sauce
- 1 (12-ounce) container refrigerated buttermilk biscuits

"This recipe is a hit with both Scouts and leaders. Other Scouters always ask for the recipe, which tied for first place in a chili cook-off at work where I even baked it using charcoal briquettes."

PREPARATION AT CAMP:

1. In a 1-gallon ziplock bag, combine flour, salt, and black pepper. Seal and shake well.
2. Add beef chunks to the bag, seal well, and toss until well coated.
3. In Dutch oven preheated over 25 coals, warm 2 tablespoons oil.
4. Add beef chunks to oven, but not the residual flour mixture. Set the remaining flour mixture aside until a later step. Cook beef until browned.
5. Add remaining 2 tablespoons oil to the oven. Once oil is hot, add the onions and mushrooms and cook until tender.
6. Add remaining ingredients, except for biscuits. Cook until heated through.
7. Stir in the remaining flour mixture, previously set aside, and cook for about 2 more minutes, or until meat sauce is slightly thickened.
8. Carefully set biscuits on top of meat sauce.
9. Bake for about 15 minutes, using 17 coals on the lid and 8 briquettes under the oven, until biscuits are a golden brown. Refresh coals if required.

REQUIRED EQUIPMENT:

12-inch camp Dutch oven
1-gallon heavy-duty ziplock bag

Richard Donegan, Lima, New York
Nundawaga District Chairman
Iroquois Trail Council

TIP: Popular brands of browning and seasoning sauce include Kitchen Bouquet and Gravy Master.

Servings: 8–10
Preparation Time: 1½ hours
Challenge Level: Moderate

Troop 281's Chicken Cordon Bleu

¼ cup (½ standard stick) butter

2 (10¾-ounce) cans Campbell's condensed cream of chicken or mushroom soup

2 (25½-ounce) bags Tyson Chicken Breast Tenders, thawed

½ pound deli-sliced ham

½ pound deli-sliced Swiss cheese

PREPARATION AT CAMP:

1. Coat bottom of Dutch oven with butter.
2. Pour 1 can soup into oven and spread evenly.
3. Layer chicken tenders, ham slices, and cheese slices evenly over soup.
4. Pour second can of soup over the top of the cheese and meat.
5. Cook for 25 minutes, using 24 coals on the lid and 12 briquettes under the oven, until the soup is bubbling and the chicken is heated through.

REQUIRED EQUIPMENT:

14-inch camp Dutch oven

George Solomon, Columbia, Pennsylvania
Assistant Scoutmaster
Troop 281, Pennsylvania Dutch Council

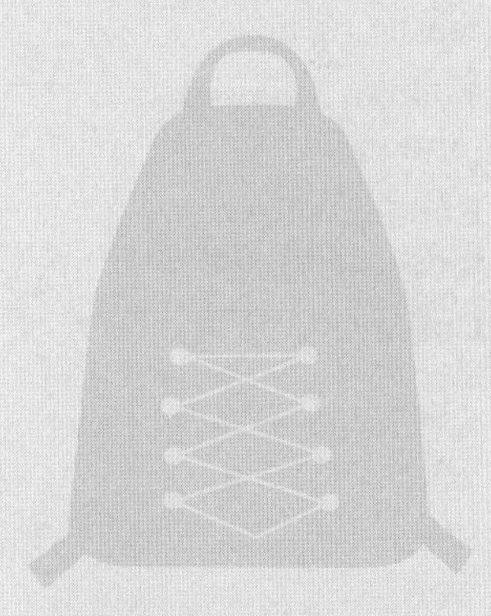

Servings: 10–12
Preparation Time: ¾ hour
Challenge Level: Easy

Easy Taco Soup

1 pound lean ground beef or turkey

2 tablespoons vegetable oil (if browning turkey)

2 (14½-ounce) cans diced tomatoes

2 (15-ounce) cans tomato sauce

2 (10½-ounce) cans low-sodium chicken broth

1 (15-ounce) can pinto beans, drained

1 (15-ounce) can black beans, drained

1 (15-ounce) can whole kernel corn

1 (1-ounce) package dry Ranch dressing mix

1 (1¼-ounce) package low-sodium taco seasoning mix

1 onion, chopped (optional)

8 ounces sliced mushrooms (optional)

Options:
Shredded cheese can be added immediately before serving.

Hot sauce is a favorite condiment.

This recipe can also be prepared in a skillet and large pot.

Servings: 10–12
Preparation Time: 1 hour
Challenge Level: Easy

"Our troop has always enjoyed winter camping in the mountains of North Carolina and Southern Virginia. Our weather may not seem very cold when compared to Minnesota or New Hampshire, but it does get pretty chilly up in our hills between November and February. Camping at that time of year brings a new appreciation for things like camp fires, warm clothes, and dry socks. The Scouts and Scouters also get into meals that really warm them on the inside, and they like the recipes to be pretty easy so as not to detract from their other activities of the day. One of our favorite recipes that meets all these requirements is Easy Taco Soup."

PREPARATION AT CAMP:

1. In Dutch oven over 32 coals, brown meat, using the vegetable oil if cooking ground turkey, which tends to be very lean.
2. Add the remainder of ingredients, including any optionals, to the pot. Stir well.
3. Cook until the troop gets hungry, but a minimum of about ½ hour.

REQUIRED EQUIPMENT:

14-inch camp Dutch oven

Keith Huffstetler, Winston-Salem, North Carolina
District Commissioner and Committee Chair
Troop 934, Piedmont District, Old Hickory Council

Dutch Oven Chicago-Style Deep Dish Pizza

1 pound sweet Italian sausage, casing removed

1 tablespoon olive oil

1 green or red bell pepper, chopped

1 medium onion, thinly sliced

4 cloves garlic, minced

8 ounces sliced fresh mushrooms

1 teaspoon dried basil

1 teaspoon dried oregano

¼ teaspoon ground black pepper

3 (13.8-ounce) containers refrigerated pizza dough

1 (15-ounce) jar pizza sauce

1 pound (4 cups) shredded mozzarella cheese

PREPARATION AT CAMP:

1. Crumble the sausage into dime-size pieces in a medium-size frying pan.
2. Cook the sausage over medium heat, stirring often until no trace of pink remains.
3. Drain grease then add olive oil, bell pepper, onion, garlic, mushrooms, basil, oregano, and black pepper. Stir.
4. Sauté until onions are translucent. Remove skillet from heat and set aside.
5. Line Dutch oven with heavy-duty aluminum foil then grease the foil.
6. In the oven, mold the pizza dough from all three containers to the shape of the bottom, leaving the outer edges of the dough thicker than the middle.
7. Spread pizza sauce over crust to within about an inch of the edge of the dough.
8. Spread sausage and sautéed vegetables evenly over the dough.
9. Cover all with cheese.
10. Bake for about 20 minutes, using 29 coals on the lid and 16 briquettes under the oven, until the cheese has completely melted and the crust is fully baked.

REQUIRED EQUIPMENT:

16-inch camp Dutch oven
Medium-size frying pan
Heavy-duty aluminum foil

George Downs, Duluth, Georgia
Assistant Scoutmaster
Troop 143, Atlanta Area Council

Servings: 10–12
Preparation Time: 1 hour
Challenge Level: Moderate

Deadly Catch Chowder

3 potatoes, peeled and chopped

1 medium onion, chopped

1 (10¾-ounce) can condensed cream of celery soup

2 cups yellow corn

1 (14½-ounce) can pink salmon, drained

2 (6-ounce) cans fancy white crabmeat, drained

¼ teaspoon salt

½ teaspoon ground black pepper

2 tablespoons diced pimientos

2 teaspoons garlic powder

2 cups heavy whipping cream

¼ cup white vinegar

1 tablespoon granulated sugar

¼ cup water

TIP:
Canned salmon can contain tiny bone fragments that you may want to remove before cooking.

Servings: 10–12
Preparation Time: 1¼ hours
Challenge Level: Moderate

"Our troop goes on a high-adventure trip to Alaska every few years. On our trip in 2006, we mixed up some soup one night with these ingredients and found that it was both filling and tasty—and all was eaten very quickly."

PREPARATION AT CAMP:

1. In cook pot, boil potatoes and onions in water for 15 minutes then drain.
2. To the pot, add celery soup, corn, salmon, crabmeat, salt, black pepper, pimentos, and garlic powder then cook over medium heat for 10 minutes.
3. Add whipping cream, vinegar, sugar, and water then bring to a boil, stirring constantly.
4. Continue to stir while boiling for 10 minutes then reduce heat, simmering for about 20 additional minutes before serving.

REQUIRED EQUIPMENT:
Medium-size cook pot

Scott Simerly, Apex, North Carolina
Scoutmaster
Troop 204, Occoneechee Council

Everyone is pitching in at this camp kitchen.
SCOTT H. SIMERLY SR.

Camp Bashore Crab Soup

"The soup was born one summer at Camp Bashore. A Scoutmaster's cook-off is held each week at summer camp, and I once won the event with an early version of this recipe. Truth be told, I never prepare it the same way twice so people don't get bored with the taste. I've used scallops and chunks of bacon that I fry in the Dutch oven prior to adding to the soup. I've even substituted diced clams for the crabmeat and made clam chowder instead."

6 medium potatoes, peeled and chopped

4 carrots, peeled and chopped

4 celery stalks, chopped

1 onion, diced

2 (15-ounce) cans tomato sauce

1 (14½-ounce) can Del Monte Diced Tomatoes with Basil, Garlic, and Oregano

2 tablespoons Old Bay spice mix

2 tablespoons dried parsley

15 ounces water

1 pound canned crabmeat with juice

PREPARATION AT CAMP:

1. Place all vegetables into cook pot.
2. Mix in tomato sauce, diced tomatoes, spices, and water.
3. Bring to a boil, then reduce heat and let simmer for 45 minutes.
4. Add crabmeat and stir well.
5. Cover and simmer for at least ½ hour or as long as an hour for fuller flavor.

REQUIRED EQUIPMENT:

Large cook pot

Derrick Tryon, Ephrata, Pennsylvania
Eagle Scout and Scoutmaster
Troop 70, Pennsylvania Dutch Council

TIP: The less-expensive brands of canned crabmeat work just fine with this recipe.

Servings: 10–12
Preparation Time: 2 hours
Challenge Level: Easy

Greater Western Reserve's Sausage Almond Dish

4 (1-pound) packages maple-flavored Italian sausage, casings removed

1 cup chopped celery

1 onion, chopped

1 (10¾-ounce) can condensed cream of mushroom soup with roasted garlic

1 (2¼-ounce) package chicken noodle soup mix

1 (1-ounce) package French onion soup mix

½ cup brown sugar

2 cups water

3 cups brown minute rice

½ cup honey

1 cup sliced almonds

PREPARATION AT CAMP:

1. Preheat Dutch oven over 25 coals.
2. Crumble and fry sausage until it is fully cooked. Do not drain oil.
3. Add celery, onion, cream of mushroom soup, dried soup mixes, and brown sugar. Mix well.
4. Add water and minute rice. Stir.
5. Bring rice mixture to a simmer, cover, and continue to cook until rice is tender, about 5 minutes.
6. Add honey and almonds. Stir, cover, and let stand 10 minutes before serving.

REQUIRED EQUIPMENT:

12-inch camp Dutch oven

John Krauss Jr., Kirtland, Ohio
Eagle Scout and Scoutmaster
Troop 562, Greater Western Reserve Council

Servings: 12–14
Preparation Time: 1 hour
Challenge Level: Easy

Snake River Pork Chops

3 potatoes, cut into ½-inch cubes

1 pound carrots, sliced into ½-inch pieces

1 large onion, chopped

Lawry's Seasoned Salt to taste

3 pounds pork chops

2 large Granny Smith apples, cored and cut into ¼-inch slices (with skins)

PREPARATION AT CAMP:

1. Layer potatoes, carrots, and onions in Dutch oven, lightly sprinkling with seasoned salt to taste as the vegetables are layered.
2. Place chops on top of vegetables.
3. Cover chops with sliced apples.
4. Bake for about 1¼ hours, using 21 coals on the lid and 11 briquettes under the oven, until meat is cooked through. Refresh coals as required.

REQUIRED EQUIPMENT:

14-inch camp Dutch oven

Delano LaGow, Oswego, Illinois
Committee Member
Troop 31, Three Fires Council

Servings: 12–14
Preparation Time: 1½ hours
Challenge Level: Easy

Chinese Railroad Workers' Dinner-in-a-Wok

3 cups long-grain white rice

6 cups water

PANS 1 AND 2:

1 pound ground turkey

8 ounces diced fresh or canned mushrooms

½ cup diced Chinese lap cheong sausage (or your favorite)

¼ cup diced green onions

1 tablespoon cooking oil

Soy sauce to taste

PAN 3:

1 pound bok choy, broccoli, or other green vegetable, cut into bite-size pieces

14 ounces firm tofu, cut into ¾-inch cubes

1 tablespoon cooking oil

Soy sauce to taste

PAN 4:

1 tablespoon cooking oil

1 pound sole or salmon fillet

1 tablespoon julienned ginger or ginger powder

¼ cup diced green onions

Soy sauce to taste

Servings: 12–14
Preparation Time: 1 hour
Challenge Level: Moderate

"This cooking method was brought to the United States in the 1860s by Chinese laborers working on the Transcontinental Railroad. Steaming the rice in the wok cooks all the dishes simultaneously, and the flavors of the dishes infuse into the rice to make a delicious meal."

PREPARATION AT CAMP:

1. Combine rice and water in wok.
2. Arrange chopsticks in a crisscross tic-tac-toe pattern on top of rice.
3. Combine all ingredients for Pans 1 and 2 in a medium-size bowl then divide the turkey-sausage mixture between the two pie pans.
4. Combine and toss all ingredients for Pan 3 in a third pie pan.
5. Spread oil in Pan 4, then add fish fillet and cover with remaining ingredients.
6. Place wok carefully over wood embers and low flame in a campfire. Use fire logs to ensure that the wok is stable. Do not cook over a roaring campfire. Otherwise, the heat will be too intense.

7. Set turkey-sausage pans on top of chopsticks at 12 and 6 o'clock positions, then place Pans 3 and 4 above the first 2 pans at the 3 and 9 o'clock positions. Cover wok tightly with domed lid.
8. After about 25 minutes, check progress of rice and meat pies. If fully cooked (with rice tender and no trace of pink in meat), remove pans from wok then remove wok from fire. If not fully cooked, return lid to wok and check at 5-minute intervals until ready.
9. Serve rice directly from the wok, and serve the sides directly from the pans.

REQUIRED EQUIPMENT:

24-inch wok with tight-fitting domed lid
4 (9-inch) aluminum pie pans
4 long chopsticks
Medium-size mixing bowl

Bruce Eng, San Francisco, California
Eagle Scout and Assistant Scoutmaster
Troop 15, San Francisco Bay Area Council

Camp cooking in a wok? Absolutely! BRUCE M. ENG

Options:

If fish is not available or not preferred, then substitute with another pan of ground meat pie above or a pound of chicken fillets cut into bite-size pieces. This is a flexible recipe. Experiment with the main ingredients.

For a late-night snack or lunch the next day, leftovers can be made into a fried rice dish by combining the remaining pan ingredients with the rice in a hot wok then stirring in 1 or 2 eggs.

TIPS:
Pans can also be prepared in advance at home. Watch the wok carefully once on the fire to be sure the rice does not overcook.

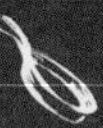

The Gourmet Scoutmaster's Chicken Scampi Alfredo

1 pound fettuccine noodles

1 (15-ounce) jar Bertolli Alfredo sauce

2 tablespoons granulated onion

2 tablespoons granulated garlic

2 tablespoons cayenne pepper

3 large boneless chicken breasts, butterflied

1 cup all-purpose flour

1 cup (2 standard sticks) salted butter

½ cup virgin olive oil

¼ cup minced garlic

5 tablespoons chopped fresh basil

Shredded Parmesan cheese to taste

Chopped fresh parsley to taste

REQUIRED EQUIPMENT:

Medium-size frying pan
Small frying pan
Medium-size cook pot
Medium-size mixing bowl
Small mixing bowl
Meat hammer

PREPARATION AT CAMP:

1. Cook fettuccine noodles in a medium-size pot according to package directions.
2. Simmer Alfredo sauce in a small pan while the remainder of the preparations are completed.
3. In a small bowl, mix granulated onion, granulated garlic, and cayenne pepper.
4. Sprinkle onion-garlic-cayenne mixture on cutting board and lay butterflied chicken on the spices.
5. Beat chicken flat with the cleated side of a meat hammer.
6. Flip meat and repeat until chicken is flattened and evenly covered in spice dust. Chicken should be hammered to less than ¼ inch thick.
7. Slice the flattened chicken into 1-inch squares.
8. Pour flour into medium-size bowl. Drop pieces into flour and lightly coat the chicken.
9. Melt butter in medium-size skillet over medium heat.
10. Pour olive oil into melted butter and let come to a simmer.
11. Add minced garlic and basil. Let the mixture simmer for about 1 minute to release the flavors into the oil.
12. Carefully drop breaded chicken pieces into the skillet, a few at a time, enough to cover the bottom of the pan.
13. Allow chicken to cook on both sides until breading is golden and meat is fully heated through.
14. Transfer chicken from oil and let drain on paper towels.
15. Repeat Steps 12, 13, and 14 with remaining chicken.
16. Pour Alfredo sauce over fettuccine noodles in the medium-size cook pot and stir.
17. Once all the chicken is drained, serve over fettuccine Alfredo and top with freshly shredded Parmesan and chopped parsley.

Servings: 12–14
Preparation Time: 1½ hours
Challenge Level: Difficult

Jason Cagle, Jacksonville, Florida
Assistant Scoutmaster
Troop 169, North Florida Council

Elk Steak on the Grill

"Start with huge expectations, add miles of hiking with loads of hunting gear, hours of glassing, and more than a few prayers spread over several days or weeks. Combine with a large dose of determination, experience, a steady trigger finger, and a pinch of luck to put the elk on the ground. Add several more hours to get it back to the truck, home, then in the freezer. Now you are ready for Elk Steak on the Grill."

12–14 elk steaks, thawed

1 (16-ounce) bottle Italian salad dressing

Lawry's Seasoned Salt to taste

Option: Recipe also works for venison, beef, pork, lamb, or chicken.

PREPARATION AT CAMP:

1. Place steaks in a large bowl.
2. Pour Italian dressing over the steaks, saturating all surfaces.
3. Cover bowl and let rest in the cooler over ice for several hours. The Italian dressing will tenderize and flavor the meat.
4. Place steaks on hot grill over coals or low flame. Season with Lawry's to taste.
5. Grill to temperature desired, minimizing flipping.

REQUIRED EQUIPMENT:

Large mixing bowl (but small enough to fit in cooler)

Glenn Larsen, Pocatello, Idaho
Assistant Scoutmaster
Troop 395, Grand Teton Council

Servings: 12–14
Preparation Time: 3 hours
Challenge Level: Easy (except for the hunting part)

Rainy Day Chicken

2 tablespoons vegetable oil

4 pounds boneless chicken, chopped into bite-size pieces

2 (16-ounce) bags frozen California-style vegetables (broccoli, carrots, and cauliflower), thawed

2 (16-ounce) jars Alfredo sauce

"We had just finished canoeing the Saint Francis River and part of the Saint John River. Not unusual for this area, we had frequent rain showers during our three-day trip. That evening, we set up camp and built a fire in a light mist, but then the heavens opened up and the mist turned into one downpour after another. With the Dutch oven sheltering the camp fire, my wife donned her rain gear and proceeded to make supper for the adults anyway. We joked that she would be better off making chicken stew because she wouldn't need to add water. The recipe came out great anyway, and that's how it earned the name 'Rainy Day Chicken.'"

PREPARATION AT CAMP:

1. Heat oil in Dutch oven over 32 coals and brown the chicken until cooked through.
2. Dump vegetables into oven then stir and cover.
3. Stir occasionally until vegetables are warm throughout, about 15 minutes. Refresh coals as required.
4. Pour Alfredo sauce over chicken-and-vegetable mixture. Stir then cover and continue to cook until thoroughly heated, about 10 additional minutes.

REQUIRED EQUIPMENT:

14-inch camp Dutch oven

David Guimond, Fort Kent, Maine
Committee Chair
Troop 189, Katahdin Area Council

Servings: 14–16
Preparation Time: 1 hour
Challenge Level: Easy

Heart of America Skillet Lasagna

2 (28-ounce) cans diced tomatoes with juice

1 (15-ounce) can tomato sauce

2½ cups water

2 tablespoons olive oil

2 onions, minced

1 teaspoon salt

4 garlic cloves, minced

½ teaspoon red pepper flakes

1 pound lean ground beef

1 pound ground pork sausage

1 (16-ounce) box lasagna noodles, broken into 2-inch pieces

¼ cup dried basil or ½ cup minced fresh basil

1 cup grated Parmesan cheese

1 (16-ounce) container ricotta cheese

Salt and ground black pepper to taste

PREPARATION AT CAMP:

1. In a medium-size bowl, combine diced tomatoes, tomato sauce, and water.
2. Heat oil in large skillet. Add the onions and salt and cook until onions are softened.
3. Stir in garlic and red pepper flakes and cook until fragrant.
4. Add ground beef and sausage and continue cooking while breaking the meat into small pieces.
5. Arrange the noodle pieces evenly over the meat.
6. If using dried basil, add it to the tomatoes in the bowl at this time and stir.
7. Pour tomato mixture over the pasta, covering the pasta completely.
8. Bring to a low boil then reduce heat to continue at a simmer, stirring occasionally until pasta is tender. Add additional water in small amounts if necessary.
9. Remove skillet from heat and stir in Parmesan and ricotta cheeses.
10. Season with salt and black pepper to taste.
11. If using fresh basil, sprinkle over the lasagna at this time.

REQUIRED EQUIPMENT:

Large frying pan
Medium-size mixing bowl

Brad Grau, Platte Woods, Missouri
Webelos Den Leader
Pack 314, Heart of America Council

Servings: 14–16
Preparation Time: 1 hour
Challenge Level: Easy

Big John's Sasquatch Succotash

3 Yukon Gold potatoes, baked at home

3 sweet potatoes, baked at home

2 medium zucchini, diced

2 tablespoons Cajun seasoning

½ cup (1 standard stick) butter

1 large onion, diced

1 yellow bell pepper, diced

1 red bell pepper, diced

1 green bell pepper, diced

3 pounds andouille sausage, sliced about ½ inch thick

2 (15-ounce) cans sweet corn, drained

Option: Regular smoked sausage is a less-spicy substitute for the andouille.

"If you're looking for new ideas for your campouts, this might be for you: a sasquatch hunt is a fun flashlight event, especially if one of the Scout leaders puts on a costume. However, a hunt should never be done on an empty stomach, so let's get a good meal in those brave Scouts before they tackle the mighty sasquatch."

PREPARATION AT HOME:

1. Bake the Yukon Gold and sweet potatoes at home.
2. Cool, package, and refrigerate until ready to use at camp.

PREPARATION AT CAMP:

1. Cut potatoes into bite-size chunks.
2. Toss zucchini with Cajun seasoning in a medium-size mixing bowl.
3. Melt butter in skillet over medium heat.
4. Sauté onion and peppers until onion is translucent.
5. Add sausage slices. Stir frequently and cook until browned.
6. Transfer seasoned zucchini to the pan and cook approximately 8 minutes, stirring frequently.
7. Add potatoes and corn and sauté until golden, about 10 to 15 minutes, stirring continuously so all the flavors mix.

REQUIRED EQUIPMENT:

Large frying pan
Medium-size mixing bowl

John Norrenberns, Mascoutah, Illinois
Cubmaster
Pack 57, Lewis & Clark Council

Servings: 14–16
Preparation Time: 1 hour
Challenge Level: Moderate

Thai Chili

"This chili started out as carnitas, a Mexican dish served on tortillas. The recipe called for using the meat but said nothing of the broth. But the broth screamed 'chili,' so I experimented and came up with 'Carnitas Chili.' My brother was into Thai food at the time, so my daughter and I tried adding soy, peanut butter, and sesame oil to a batch, and 'Thai Chili' was born."

3 pounds pork pot roast, with bone

4 cups chicken broth

1 large onion, chopped

1 (7-ounce) can chipotle peppers in adobo sauce

2 tablespoons dried oregano

2 bay leaves

1 teaspoon ground cumin

1 tablespoon minced garlic

2 tablespoons dried cilantro or dried parsley

Water, enough to cover meat

4 (15-ounce) cans beans (a mix of your favorites), drained

2 tablespoons soy sauce

¼ cup peanut butter

1 teaspoon sesame oil

Salt to taste

Optional: Shredded cheese and sour cream

PREPARATION AT CAMP:

1. Place roast in large stockpot.
2. Add broth, onion, chipotle peppers, oregano, bay leaves, cumin, garlic, and cilantro or parsley, followed by enough water to just cover meat.
3. Cook for 2 to 3 hours at a low boil until meat falls from the bone.
4. Remove bay leaves and discard.
5. Transfer pork to tray, discard bone, and shred meat.
6. Move shredded meat back to the broth in the pot then add beans, soy sauce, peanut butter, and sesame oil. Mix well then add salt to taste.
7. Warm over medium flame until heated throughout.
8. Serve with optional shredded cheese or sour cream.

TIP: If a member of your group has a nut allergy, simply leave out the soy, peanut butter, and sesame oil, and you'll have the original Carnitas Chili recipe.

REQUIRED EQUIPMENT:

Large cook pot

Richard Wallace, Bay City, Michigan
Adviser
Venture Crew 7100, Lake Huron Area Council

Servings: 14–16
Preparation Time: 3 hours
Challenge Level: Moderate

5-Gallon Spaghetti

1 pound lean ground beef

1 pound Italian sausage, skinned and separated, like ground beef

1 pound spaghetti pasta

2 teaspoons salt

¼ cup extra-virgin olive oil, plus a little extra for boiling spaghetti

⅛ cup minced garlic

3 tablespoons chopped fresh basil

3 tablespoons chopped fresh parsley

3 tablespoons chopped fresh oregano

4 whole bay leaves

1 large onion, cut into ½-inch wedges

1½ cups sliced fresh baby portabella mushrooms

3 large green bell peppers, sliced ½ inch thick

1 (10-ounce) jar sun-dried tomato pesto, drained

1 (12-ounce) can Hunt's tomato paste

2 (29-ounce) cans Hunt's tomato sauce

2 (14½-ounce) cans stewed tomatoes, chopped

½ cup whole or halved black olives, pitless

1¼ cups water

Fresh grated Parmesan to taste

"Despite the name, this recipe makes less than half that. I just named it '5-Gallon' because it seems like it's that much."

PREPARATION AT CAMP:

1. Brown beef and sausage together in skillet. Drain grease and set aside.
2. Boil spaghetti noodles as instructed on package in a medium-size cook pot. Add salt and a little olive oil to the water for taste and to keep the noodles from sticking together. Cook the pasta for only about three-quarters of the usual time. It will finish cooking with the sauce in a later step. Drain pasta and set aside.
3. Over medium heat, pour ¼ cup olive oil into a large cook pot and mix in garlic, basil, parsley, oregano, and bay leaves.
4. Let the oil come to a simmer. Add onion, mushrooms, and bell peppers then stir.
5. Once onions become translucent, pour in pesto, tomato paste, tomato sauce, and stewed tomatoes. Stir until vegetables and spices have fully blended.
6. Add olives, water, and previously cooked meat. Let simmer on medium-low for 15 minutes, stirring every 5 minutes.
7. Add partially cooked pasta to spaghetti sauce. Stir until the sauce and pasta are thoroughly mixed. Cover and continue to cook at low temperature for 30 minutes, stirring about every 10 minutes.
8. Serve with fresh grated Parmesan.

REQUIRED EQUIPMENT:

Large cook pot (at least 12-quart capacity)
Medium-size cook pot
Medium-size frying pan

Jason Cagle, Jacksonville, Florida
Assistant Scoutmaster
Troop 169, North Florida Council

Servings: 16–18
Preparation Time: 1¼ hours
Challenge Level: Difficult

Okee Tuklo Lasagna

1 pound spicy hot Italian sausage, crumbled

1 pound lean ground beef

1 onion, chopped

1 teaspoon garlic powder

1 pound frozen chopped spinach, thawed

1 (26-ounce) can condensed cream of mushroom soup

1 (26-ounce) jar spaghetti sauce (your favorite)

2 teaspoons Italian herb seasoning

1 (9-ounce) package no-boil lasagna noodles

3 ounces grated Parmesan cheese

2 (8-ounce) packages Velveeta shredded cheese

1 pound (4 cups) grated mozzarella cheese

Optional: Garlic bread

PREPARATION AT CAMP:

1. In Dutch oven preheated over 32 coals, brown sausage and beef with the onion.
2. Place meat-onion mixture in a large bowl and drain excess grease from oven.
3. To the bowl, add garlic powder, spinach, soup, spaghetti sauce, and Italian seasoning. Mix well.
4. Place a layer of noodles on bottom of oven. Break noodles as required to fit the shape of the oven.
5. Cover noodles with about half the meat sauce followed by about a third of each of the cheeses.
6. Repeat Steps 4 and 5 to create one more layer.
7. Cover the second layer of sauce and cheese with a final layer of noodles.
8. Completely cover the final layer of noodles with the remaining cheese.
9. Bake for 1 hour, using 21 coals on the lid and 11 briquettes under the oven, until the lasagna is bubbling and the cheese cap has begun to brown. Refresh coals as required.
10. Serve with optional garlic bread.

REQUIRED EQUIPMENT:

14-inch camp Dutch oven
Large mixing bowl

Kristen Swank, Winnsboro, Texas
Crew Adviser and Okee Tuklo District Training Chair
Crew 42, East Texas Area Council

Servings: 16–18
Preparation Time: 1¾ hours
Challenge Level: Easy

California Chicken Casserole

4 (10¾-ounce) cans condensed cream of mushroom soup

4 cups milk

1 (4½-pound) bag frozen broccoli, carrots, and cauliflower florets, thawed

2 (22-ounce) bags Tyson Grilled & Ready frozen chicken breasts, thawed and chopped

4 cups minute brown rice

6 cups shredded Swiss cheese

PREPARATION AT CAMP:

1. Combine all ingredients in Dutch oven except for 1½ cups shredded cheese. Stir well.
2. Top with the remaining cheese.
3. Bake for about 1¼ hours, using 21 coals on the lid and 11 briquettes under the oven. Refresh coals as required.

REQUIRED EQUIPMENT:

14-inch camp Dutch oven

Jason Cagle, Jacksonville, Florida
Assistant Scoutmaster
Troop 169, North Florida Council

"Hey look! We didn't burn dinner!" *SCOTT H. SIMERLY SR.*

Servings: 18–20
Preparation Time: 1½ hours
Challenge Level: Easy

Campfire Chili

"Tastes great on a cold night."

1 pound lean ground beef
1 pound cubed stew meat
1 pound spicy pork sausage, crumbled
1 pound bacon, cut into squares
1 tablespoon fresh minced garlic
1 onion, chopped
1 (26-ounce) jar Ragu Roasted Garlic spaghetti sauce
1 (15-ounce) can chili beans, drained
1 (15-ounce) can kidney beans, drained
1 (15-ounce) can pinto beans, drained
3 (10-ounce) cans Ro*Tel diced tomatoes and green chilies
2½ teaspoons ground cumin
2½ teaspoons ground ancho pepper
1 teaspoon chili powder
1 cup white or red grape juice
1 pound turkey links

PREPARATION AT CAMP:

1. Brown beef, stew meat, sausage, bacon, garlic, and onion in Dutch oven preheated over 32 coals until onions are translucent.
2. Carefully drain any grease.
3. Add remaining ingredients to the oven. Stir well.
4. Remove 10 coals from under the oven and simmer for at least 3 hours, stirring occasionally. Refresh coals as needed.

REQUIRED EQUIPMENT:

14-inch camp Dutch oven

Jeff Schmid, Loveland, Colorado
Committee Member
Troop 9, Longs Peak Council

Servings: 20–22
Preparation Time: 3½ hours
Challenge Level: Easy

Buried Turkey with Pineapple Stuffing

½ cup (1 standard stick) butter, softened

1 (15-pound) whole turkey, thawed and cleaned

PINEAPPLE STUFFING:

2 (1-pound) loaves white, French, or honey whole wheat bread

2 (20-ounce) cans crushed pineapple in heavy syrup (do not drain)

2 medium onions, diced

4 stalks celery, thinly sliced

1 tablespoon ground cinnamon

2 teaspoons sage

1 teaspoon ground black pepper

1 tablespoon salt

5 large eggs

1 cup milk

PREPARATION IN CAMP:

1. Smear softened butter over the entire bird.
2. Pack turkey in burlap sack, cheesecloth, or brown paper bag then wrap it tightly with 5 layers of heavy-duty foil.
3. Secure a loop of bailing wire around the turkey, leaving several feet of excess wire to allow the turkey to be pulled from the ground once it has finished cooking.
4. In soil that isn't excessively moist, dig a pit with a diameter and depth about 2 times the width and length of the turkey. The pit should be at least 2 feet deep.
5. Inside the pit, burn about 10 average-size pieces of firewood, allowing 2 hours for the embers to develop.
6. Add about 10 more pieces of firewood and allow them to burn for an additional hour.
7. With the wood fire burned down and the embers white hot, evenly pour about 15 pounds of charcoal over the wood embers.
8. Once the charcoal becomes ashed over, spread the coals to the sides of the pit with the shovel so that only about 1 layer of briquettes remains in the middle of the pit.
9. Place the bird in the center of the pit and use the remainder of the coals pushed to the sides to cover the bird.
10. Bury the turkey and coals under about 1 foot of loose dirt. Don't firmly pack the dirt down. Be sure the end of the bailing wire protrudes from the top of the pit.
11. Allow the turkey to cook for 5 to 6 hours.

Servings: 18–20
Preparation Time: 10 hours
Challenge Level: Difficult

12. About an hour before the turkey finishes cooking, begin to prepare the stuffing by tearing the bread into pieces an inch or so on a side.
13. Place bread in large bowl then add crushed pineapple, diced onions, celery, and all the seasonings. Toss until well mixed.
14. In a medium-size bowl, beat the eggs with milk.
15. Slowly pour the egg mixture over the bread to evenly coat. The bread should absorb the liquid. If the mixture seems too dry, add a little extra milk or water.
16. Pour stuffing into Dutch oven and bake for 45 minutes, using 17 coals on the lid and 8 briquettes under the oven.
17. Once the bird is ready, remove the top layer of dirt with the shovel and pull the turkey from the pit.
18. Carefully remove the wire, foil, and burlap from the bird. Serve with dressing.

REQUIRED EQUIPMENT:

12-inch camp Dutch oven
Clean burlap sack, cheesecloth, or large plain brown paper grocery bag (no inks)
Heavy-duty aluminum foil
6 feet uncoated metal braided wire
About 20 average-size pieces of firewood
15 pounds charcoal
Large mixing bowl
Medium-size mixing bowl
Shovel

Marc Robinson, Canton, Michigan
Eagle Scout and Assistant Scoutmaster
Troop 854, Great Lakes Council

Caution:

Use a food thermometer to be certain the turkey has fully cooked before serving.

Caution:

Pit must be free of peat, tree roots, and other matter that might otherwise ignite and spread laterally underground.

Camp Mack Crab Alfredo Pasta

"This is one of my favorite recipes."

PREPARATION AT CAMP:

1. Boil and drain bow-tie noodles in large cook pot.
2. Break crabmeat into small pieces.
3. Add crabmeat, Alfredo sauce, peas, salt, and black pepper to the pot.
4. Stir and simmer on low heat until heated through.

REQUIRED EQUIPMENT:

Large cook pot

Derrick Tryon, Ephrata, Pennsylvania
Eagle Scout and Scoutmaster
Troop 70, Pennsylvania Dutch Council

Servings			
8	**16**	**24**	**Ingredients**
1	2	3	1-pound bags bow-tie noodles
½ pound	1 pound	1½ pounds	imitation crabmeat
1	2	3	15-ounce jars Bertolli Alfredo sauce
1	2	3	1-pound bags frozen peas, thawed
			salt and ground black pepper to taste

Servings: 8–24
Preparation Time: ½ hour
Challenge Level: Easy

Asian Vagabond Foil Cookin'

"Introduce your fellow Scouts to an international world of flavors with this vagabond meal. Don't be afraid to experiment with the ingredients either—the combinations are endless and delicious."

PREPARATION AT CAMP:

1. On each of eight 18 x 18-inch sheets of heavy-duty aluminum foil, layer ingredients in the order listed.
2. Seal packets very tightly by folding the edges over repeatedly. Attempt to make the packets "airtight."
3. If packets have been customized, put name of each owner on the foil with a marker.
4. Heat on a grill over medium heat or over a low campfire for about 20 minutes.

REQUIRED EQUIPMENT:

Heavy-duty aluminum foil (18 inches wide)

TIPS:

Foil cooking may appear simple, but it can be challenging to reach the balance between fully cooked meat and tender vegetables. The following tips will help to ensure consistently great results:

- When using uncooked meat, place it at bottom of packet, closest to heat source.
- It is crucial to the cooking process that you seal the packs tightly to trap steam. A packet that loses too much moisture will cook unevenly or char.
- Do not place packets over intense heat, which will burn the contents. Instead, cook the packets on a grill at medium heat or over a low campfire, never in direct contact with the flame.

Tim Conners, Statesboro, Georgia
Assistant Scoutmaster
Troop 340, Coastal Empire Council

Christine Conners, Statesboro, Georgia
Committee Member and Merit Badge Counselor
Troop 340, Coastal Empire Council

Servings: 8–24
Preparation Time: ¾ hour
Challenge Level: Moderate

Servings			
8	**16**	**24**	**Ingredients**
½ cup	1 cup	1½ cups	peanut oil
2 pounds	4 pounds	6 pounds	uncooked peeled shrimp or extra-firm tofu
1	2	3	11.8-ounce jars Kikkoman Teriyaki Baste & Glaze
1	2	3	bell peppers, cut into thin slices
1	2	3	6-ounce bags sliced almonds
1	2	3	heads bok choy, trimmed and chopped
1	2	3	sweet onions, cut into thin wedges
½ pound	1 pound	1½ pounds	snow peas
1	2	3	20-ounce cans crushed pineapple in heavy syrup (do not drain)
1	2	3	heads broccoli, cut into quartered florets

Sawtooth Shrimp Étouffée

"This is a version of my trail recipe that I modified for use in camp. The title was inspired by the Sawtooth Mountains of Idaho, where my husband and I did much of our backpacking."

PREPARATION AT CAMP:

1. Bring water to a boil in large cook pot.
2. Add onion, bell pepper, celery, bay leaves, chili powder, bouillon cubes, and salt. Stir and reduce heat.
3. In a separate large pot, cook rice according to package directions.
4. Once vegetables have simmered for about 35 minutes, add shrimp and stir. Continue to cook over low heat, about 5 additional minutes, or until shrimp turns fully pink.
5. Fluff rice once it has finished cooking, blending in recommended salt and butter according to package directions.
6. Remove bay leaves and spoon shrimp mixture over rice, serving in bowls.

TIP:
The liquid remaining in the cook pot containing the shrimp makes for an excellent soup.

REQUIRED EQUIPMENT:
2 large cook pots

Servings: 8–24
Preparation Time: 1 hour
Challenge Level: Moderate

Lori Neumann, Darlington, Wisconsin
Committee Member
Troop 125, Blackhawk Area Council

Servings			
8	**16**	**24**	**Ingredients**
2 cups	4 cups	6 cups	water
2	4	6	large onions, chopped
2	4	6	bell peppers, chopped
4	8	12	stalks celery, chopped
6	12	18	bay leaves
2 teaspoons	4 teaspoons	2 tablespoons	chili powder
2	4	6	beef bouillon cubes
2 teaspoons	4 teaspoons	2 tablespoons	salt
2 cups	4 cups	6 cups	brown rice
2 pounds	4 pounds	6 pounds	peeled raw shrimp, fresh or frozen
			water, salt, and butter according to rice package instructions

Old Drum Ranch Chicken Cheese Pasta

"We had gone on a practice hike at Old Drum Ranch. Stopped at a creek to filter some water. We were packing up the bottles on a small cliff about 30 feet above the river when one of the boys took his sleeping bag out of his pack to make room for his bottles. Well, he didn't understand the law of gravity and let the sleeping bag roll off the cliff, directly into the fast-moving river. He yelled, 'My sleeping bag is floating away!' By the time the rest of us got over to have a look, his bag was bobbing down the rapid. The boys ran nearly a mile downstream to try to catch it. The bag ended up getting caught on a rock in the middle of the river. We had to form a human chain to extract it. The previously ultra-lightweight bag now weighed about 20 pounds. The Scout was overwrought, worried, and embarrassed. He definitely needed some comforting and some comfort food. This recipe happened to be on the menu that night, and it really did the trick in raising his spirits. It will always be tied to that story, even years after this future Eagle Scout discovered how gravity works."

4 pounds skinless, boneless chicken breasts

8 cups chicken broth

2 pounds regular spaghetti noodles

1 bell pepper, diced

1 small onion, diced

2 (10¾-ounce) cans condensed cream of mushroom soup

1 (4-ounce) jar pimientos

32 ounces Cheez Whiz cheese dip

PREPARATION IN CAMP:

1. In a large cook pot, boil the chicken in the broth for about 20 minutes, until no trace of pink remains in the meat.
2. Remove chicken from the broth and carefully cut into bite-size pieces. Set aside.
3. Cook the spaghetti noodles in the leftover chicken broth, adding the diced bell pepper and onion about halfway through the pasta's cooking time.
4. Once the noodles become tender, lower heat then add the mushroom soup, pimientos, Cheez Whiz, and previously cooked chicken to the pot.
5. Stir thoroughly for a couple of minutes. Remove from heat then serve.

REQUIRED EQUIPMENT:

Large cook pot (at least 8-quart capacity)

Servings: 22–24
Preparation Time: 1 hour
Challenge Level: Easy

David Visser, Hurst, Texas
Assistant Scoutmaster
Troop 340, Longhorn Council

Veggie Lasagna

LASAGNA FILLING:

3 (45-ounce) jars pasta sauce (your favorite)

1 (30-ounce) container ricotta cheese

2 pounds zucchini or summer squash, chopped

6 Roma tomatoes, chopped

2 tablespoons Italian seasoning

4 cloves garlic, minced

1 (8-ounce) jar sliced mushrooms, drained

1 (9-ounce) box frozen chopped spinach (do not drain)

24 ounces regular lasagna noodles

1 pound (4 cups) shredded mozzarella cheese

1 (8-ounce) container Parmesan cheese

Servings: 22–24
Preparation Time: 1¼ hours
Challenge Level: Easy

PREPARATION IN CAMP:

1. Prepare lasagna filling in a large bowl by combining pasta sauce, ricotta cheese, squash, tomatoes, Italian seasoning, garlic, mushrooms, and spinach.
2. Spread a thin layer of filling on bottom of Dutch oven.
3. Cover bottom of oven with a single layer of uncooked lasagna noodles, breaking the noodles as required to fit the shape of the oven.
4. Add about a quarter of the remaining filling to fully cover the noodles. To the top of the filling, add a quarter of the mozzarella and Parmesan cheeses.
5. Repeat Steps 3 and 4 three more times, ending with the remainder of mozzarella and Parmesan cheeses on top.
6. Bake for about 1 hour, using 26 coals on the lid and 13 briquettes under the oven, until the lasagna is fully heated through. Refresh coals as required.

REQUIRED EQUIPMENT:

16-inch camp Dutch oven
Large mixing bowl

Tim Conners, Statesboro, Georgia
Assistant Scoutmaster
Troop 340, Coastal Empire Council

Christine Conners, Statesboro, Georgia
Committee Member and Merit Badge Counselor
Troop 340, Coastal Empire Council

Lodge 550 Tortellini Soup

"This is a family recipe that I decided to try out on my Order of the Arrow boys. It makes for a really great wintertime soup, but I prepare it anytime of the year."

½ cup (1 standard stick) butter

4 cloves garlic, chopped

3 cups finely chopped celery

2 cups finely chopped carrots

1 large onion, finely chopped

8 cups chicken broth

3 (29-ounce) cans tomato sauce

6 cups water

3 (12-ounce) packages dried cheese-filled tortellini

¼ teaspoon ground cinnamon

1 (8-ounce) container grated Parmesan and Romano cheese blend

Salt and ground black pepper to taste

PREPARATION AT CAMP:

1. Melt butter in large pot and add garlic, celery, carrots, and onion. Stir and sauté for 20 minutes.
2. Add chicken broth, tomato sauce, and water. Stir, then heat to boiling.
3. Pour in tortellini, then cover and cook for about 20 minutes, until pasta is tender.
4. Stir in ground cinnamon and grated cheese.
5. Add salt and black pepper to taste then serve.

REQUIRED EQUIPMENT:

Large cook pot with lid (at least 10-quart capacity)

Beverly Jo Antonini, Morgantown, West Virginia
Assistant Scoutmaster
Troop 49, Mountaineer Area Council

Troop 340's campfire and tarp shelter at summer camp. *TIM CONNERS*

Servings: 22–24
Preparation Time: 1¼ hours
Challenge Level: Easy

Scoutmaster's Seafood Jambalaya

¼ cup vegetable oil

1 pound andouille sausage, sliced ½ inch thick

1 pound chicken, chopped into bite-size pieces

2 yellow onions, diced

1 bunch celery, diced

4 bell peppers (2 green, 1 red, and 1 yellow), diced

3 cloves garlic, minced

5 cups water

2 (14½-ounce) cans chicken broth

4 cups Zatarain's Enriched Natural Parboiled Extra Long Grain rice

3 tablespoons Worcestershire sauce

1 cup orange juice

1½ pounds small button mushrooms, quartered

4 large ripe tomatoes, chopped

2 pounds okra, cut into thin slices

2 pounds mixed bite-size seafood (calamari, scallops, crab, your choice)

2 pounds raw peeled shrimp

1 tablespoon cayenne pepper or Cajun seasoning

1 teaspoon ground black pepper

1 teaspoon ground white pepper

¼ cup gumbo filé powder

Salt to taste

PREPARATION AT CAMP:

1. Add vegetable oil to Dutch oven and heat over 32 coals; then brown the sausage and chicken until meat is fully cooked.
2. Add onions, celery, bell peppers, and garlic then sauté until vegetables are soft.
3. Add water and chicken broth to the oven.
4. Bring to a gentle boil, then add rice, Worcestershire sauce, orange juice, mushrooms, tomatoes, and okra to the oven.
5. Remove about 10 coals from under the oven and simmer for about 30 minutes with the lid on, stirring every 5 minutes or so. Refresh coals if required.
6. Meanwhile, in a large pot, steam seafood and shrimp until shrimp turns fully pink.
7. Add seafood to jambalaya along with remaining seasonings.
8. Stir gently for a couple of minutes, then serve.

REQUIRED EQUIPMENT:

Deep 14-inch camp Dutch oven
Large cook pot with steaming basket

Barry Moore, Tampa, Florida
Former District Chairman
Lake Region District, Gulf Ridge Council

Option: Goes great with Scoutmaster's Corn Bread, also in this book.

Servings: 22–24
Preparation Time: 1½ hours
Challenge Level: Difficult

Parris Island Turkey Chili

"One year, I was asked to prepare a non-beef chili for the upcoming Camporee to be held at Parris Island, South Carolina. I had no idea what to do or what to include, so I went to the Internet and printed off several recipes. I studied them and came up with my own. I did not have time to test it in advance. I stopped on the way to the Camporee to shop for food, but upon entering the store, I realized I had left my grocery list at home. I just roamed around looking for anything remotely associated with a chili recipe and began to throw things into my shopping cart. When it came time to prepare the food at the Camporee, I sliced and diced and sautéed and prayed that my chili would turn out to at least be edible and not make anyone sick. At dinnertime, the boys went through the food line and received a serving each of my chili and the Scoutmaster's. Seconds were offered. A line quickly formed in front of my chili stand and not one in front of the other—until I ran out."

4 pounds ground turkey

¾ cup olive oil

1 Vidalia or regular sweet onion, finely diced

1 large bell pepper, finely diced

4 (28-ounce) cans diced tomatoes

6 (16-ounce) cans light red kidney beans, drained

2 (10-ounce) cans Ro*Tel Hot Diced Tomatoes with Habañeros

3 (11-ounce) cans shoe-peg white corn, drained

1 tablespoon dried cilantro

2 tablespoons ground cumin

2 tablespoons salt

3 tablespoons course ground black pepper

Optional: French bread or your favorite

PREPARATION AT CAMP:

1. Preheat Dutch oven over 40 coals and brown ground turkey in olive oil. Separate the chunks of turkey into small pieces while browning.
2. Add onion and bell pepper then sauté until tender. Do not overcook.
3. Add diced tomatoes, kidney beans, diced tomatoes with habañeros, corn, and all the spices. Stir until fully mixed.
4. Continue to cook until hot and bubbling, then remove about 10 coals from under the oven and simmer for approximately 2 hours, stirring occasionally. Be careful not to burn the chili, checking often. Refresh coals as required.
5. Serve with an optional chunk of your favorite bread.

REQUIRED EQUIPMENT:

16-inch camp Dutch oven

Servings: 22–24
Preparation Time: 2¾ hours
Challenge Level: Moderate

Lanny Rhodes, Savannah, Georgia
Assistant Council Commissioner
Coastal Empire Council

Coastal Empire Low-Country Boil

"This eclectic and multidimensional recipe is a longtime favorite down here in the Coastal Empire. A common mistake made with low-country boils is over- or undercooking the ingredients. So the trick in making the recipe great lies in the timing."

1 (6-ounce) tin Old Bay seasoning

6 pounds Polska kielbasa sausage, cut into 1-inch-thick pieces

6 pounds whole small red potatoes, scrubbed

20 ears corn, husks and silks removed, each cut into 2 pieces

6 pounds raw shrimp in the shell

YOUR CHOICE OF CONDIMENTS:

Lemons, sliced into wedges

Melted butter

Tarter sauce

Tabasco sauce

Coarse-ground mustard

Cocktail sauce

Any remaining Old Bay seasoning

Option: When money is no obstacle, crab legs and crawdads are often added to the boil a few minutes before the shrimp.

Servings: 24–26
Preparation Time: 1¾ hours
Challenge Level: Moderate

PREPARATION AT CAMP:

1. Fill stockpot half-full with water and bring to a boil over high heat on a sturdy propane cooker. Keep in mind that it can take a long time to bring 10 gallons of water to boiling.
2. Add Old Bay to the hot water, reserving a small amount of the spice as optional additional seasoning once the food is served.
3. Add kielbasa sausage and continue to boil for about 20 minutes.
4. Add potatoes and boil for an additional 15 minutes.
5. Next, add corn and boil for 10 more minutes.
6. Finally, add shrimp and cook for 2 to 3 minutes if shrimp is thawed, or about 5 minutes if shrimp is frozen. Shrimp is ready once it turns pink throughout.

TIPS:

- Having a hose handy to dilute and cool down the cooking water afterward will help to speed up cleanup. Otherwise, the pot can take hours to cool on its own.
- This recipe can be easily adapted to any size group using the following formula per person: ¼ pound kielbasa, ¼ pound shrimp, 1 potato, and 1 or 2 half-ears of corn.

7. Immediately remove the basket from the pot once the shrimp turns pink. This final step is important because leaving the shrimp to boil any longer will turn them rubbery.
8. Allow basket to drain for a moment then carefully dump the food on a table covered with a clean plastic tablecloth.
9. Serve with condiments and a lot of paper towels.

REQUIRED EQUIPMENT:

80-quart stockpot with perforated basket
Very sturdy high-BTU propane cooker
Plastic tablecloth

Tim Conners, Statesboro, Georgia
Assistant Scoutmaster
Troop 340, Coastal Empire Council

Christine Conners, Statesboro, Georgia
Committee Member and Merit Badge Counselor
Troop 340, Coastal Empire Council

Low-country boil: it's perfect for large crowds.
KROFTON OWEN

Caution:

The pot, when full of water and food for this recipe, will weigh about 100 pounds. That much heat and mass makes for a potentially hazardous situation. It is critical that your propane cooker is stout enough to handle the weight and stable enough to not tip while cooking. Never attempt to move a pot loaded with scalding water. Allow the water to cool first. Otherwise, the sloshing liquid can burn large areas of skin. It is also prudent to ask for assistance when moving a very large pot full of water, one person to a handle, to avoid a strain-related injury.

Troop 169 Loaded Potato Soup

12 large baked potatoes

½ cup (2 standard sticks) salted butter

16 ounces light sour cream

2 quarts heavy whipping cream

2 tablespoons ground sea salt

3 tablespoons ground white pepper

¼ cup Worcestershire sauce

8 ounces (2 cups) shredded cheddar cheese

½ cup real bacon bits

3 bunches chives

Options:

Use half-and-half in place of the whipping cream to cut some of the fat.

Potatoes can also be baked at camp in Dutch ovens or in foil over coals.

Servings: 24–26
Preparation Time: 1 hour
Challenge Level: Difficult

"This is the 'Mona Lisa' of all my recipes. It has won multiple awards: Best-of-Show All-Categories in a local cook-off in Georgia for two years in a row, First Place twice in the Scoutmaster cook-off at Council Camporees, among others. I'd been making this soup every Thanksgiving and Christmas for the family dinners until a couple of years ago, when I wasn't able to get around to it. I was nearly banished from all future family holiday get-togethers."

PREPARATION AT HOME:

1. Bake potatoes in oven or microwave.
2. Cool and cut into quarters lengthwise.
3. Slice potato meat from the skins. Discard skins.
4. Cut potato meat into ¼-inch to ½-inch chunks.
5. Refrigerate until ready to use at camp.

PREPARATION AT CAMP:

1. In large stockpot over medium heat, melt butter and blend in sour cream and whipping cream. Let warm till the top froths.
2. Stir in salt, white pepper, and Worcestershire sauce.
3. Add cheddar, a little at a time to keep it from clumping while it melts.
4. Finally, add bacon bits, chives, and cooked potato chunks and stir.
5. Reduce heat, simmering over low flame, covered, for about 40 minutes, stirring every 5 minutes. Be careful not to let the solids collect at the bottom while the soup is simmering, or it will burn and ruin the soup. You have to keep an eye on this one.

REQUIRED EQUIPMENT:
Large cook pot

Jason Cagle, Jacksonville, Florida
Assistant Scoutmaster
Troop 169, North Florida Council

Grand Teton Enchilada Casserole

"This recipe is very forgiving. If someone in your pack or troop wants to hold the olives or add more chiles, it still works."

3 pounds lean ground beef

2 onions, chopped

30 corn tortillas

3 pounds shredded pepper Jack cheese

2 (19-ounce) cans green enchilada sauce

3 (3.8-ounce) cans sliced olives, drained

4 (7-ounce) cans green chiles

1 (24-ounce) container sour cream

4 (16-ounce) cans refried beans

PREPARATION AT CAMP:

1. In Dutch oven preheated over 37 coals, brown the ground beef.
2. Add the onions and sauté until translucent.
3. Transfer beef-onion mixture to a medium-size bowl. Remove oven from coals.
4. Cover bottom of oven with 12 tortillas, evenly arranged in 2 layers.
5. Reserve 2 cups cheese for a later step.
6. Build 3 layers by dividing the remaining ingredients equally among the layers, topping each layer with 6 tortillas before moving on to the next. You should end with a layer of 6 tortillas.
7. Top the final layer of tortillas with the 2 cups cheese previously set aside.
8. Cook for about 1 hour, using 25 coals on the lid and 12 briquettes under the oven. Refresh coals as needed.
9. Remove lid and let cool for about 10 minutes to set the cheese for easier serving.

REQUIRED EQUIPMENT:

16-inch camp Dutch oven
Medium-size bowl

Betty Klements, Shelley, Idaho
Cubmaster
Pack 161, Grand Teton Council

Servings: 26–28
Preparation Time: 2 hours
Challenge Level: Easy

Mountaineer Camp Meatball Hoagies

MEATBALLS:
8 pounds lean ground beef

¾ cup grated Parmesan cheese

3 tablespoons dried basil

2 tablespoons dried oregano

2 tablespoons chopped garlic

1 small onion, finely chopped

3 eggs

2 cups Progresso Italian bread crumbs

1 (12-ounce) can evaporated milk

Olive oil to fry meatballs

SAUCE:
4 (10¾-ounce) cans condensed cream of mushroom soup

2 (29-ounce) cans tomato sauce

1¾ pounds (7 cups) shredded mozzarella cheese

30 hoagie buns

Servings: 30
Preparation Time: 1¾ hours
Challenge Level: Moderate

"This recipe came from having leftover meatballs while fixing hoagies for some hungry Scouts. Now it's a regular part of Saturday's lunch."

PREPARATION AT CAMP:

1. Prepare meatballs by combining beef, Parmesan cheese, basil, oregano, garlic, onion, eggs, bread crumbs, and evaporated milk in a large bowl. With clean hands, mix well.
2. Form into 90 meatballs, firmly pressing together the meat mixture.
3. Heat olive oil in a large frying pan and brown meatballs in batches, stirring frequently. Meatballs are not cooked through on this step. The browning process is used to intensify the flavor, and the meatballs will finish cooking during simmering in Step 5.
4. In large cooking pot, combine cream of mushroom soup and tomato sauce.
5. Add meatballs to the pot then simmer for 1 hour.
6. Serve meatballs sprinkled with mozzarella cheese on hoagie buns.

REQUIRED EQUIPMENT:
Large cook pot (at least 10-quart capacity)
Large frying pan
Large mixing bowl

Beverly Jo Antonini, Morgantown, West Virginia
Assistant Scoutmaster
Troop 49, Mountaineer Area Council

TIPS:
- To produce meatballs of the proper size for this recipe, they should fit within the circle formed by your middle finger when it touches your thumb.
- To accommodate various appetites and to reduce waste, cut and serve hoagies in halves.

Mom's Broccoli Salad

"This comes from my mother, who always could do amazing things with this awesome vegetable. With recipes like this, she never had to coax me into eating my greens."

1 pound bacon

DRESSING:
1 cup mayonnaise

½ cup granulated sugar

2 tablespoons white vinegar

3 bunches broccoli

1 red onion, diced

4 ounces (1 cup) shredded Swiss cheese

PREPARATION AT CAMP:

1. In frying pan, cook bacon until crispy.
2. Place bacon on paper towels to drain, then crumble the bacon.
3. Combine dressing ingredients in ziplock bag. Seal the bag then mush to mix.
4. Using only the broccoli florets, and not the thick stems, chop florets into small ½-inch pieces.
5. Add broccoli florets, onion, cheese, and cooked bacon to the bag and shake to coat.
6. Place bag in a cooler over ice to chill for an hour or so before serving.

REQUIRED EQUIPMENT:

Medium-size frying pan
1 (1-gallon) heavy-duty ziplock bag

Tim Conners, Statesboro, Georgia
Assistant Scoutmaster
Troop 340, Coastal Empire Council

Servings: 8–10
Preparation Time: 1¼ hours
Challenge Level: Easy

Summer Vegetable Bake

2 medium zucchini, sliced into pieces about ¾ inch thick

6 medium yellow squash, sliced into pieces about ¾ inch thick

2 medium yellow onions, sliced into pieces ½ inch thick

2 (14½-ounce) cans seasoned diced tomatoes (do not drain)

2 tablespoons butter

Salt and ground black pepper to taste

"I had been telling a friend about how good this recipe was. So one summer night, while I was at his house, I decided to make it for him. I didn't have a Dutch oven with me, and the grill was already full of meat, with no room left. So I prepared it by double-wrapping a huge piece of foil around the vegetables and cooking it over coals on his driveway."

PREPARATION AT CAMP:

1. Place sliced zucchini, yellow squash, and onions in Dutch oven.
2. Pour cans of diced tomatoes, with juice, over the vegetables.
3. Top with thin slices of butter.
4. Bake for about 35 minutes, using 17 coals on the lid and 8 briquettes under the oven, until all vegetables are tender.
5. Add salt and black pepper to taste.

REQUIRED EQUIPMENT:

12-inch camp Dutch oven

Scott Simerly, Apex, North Carolina
Scoutmaster
Troop 204, Occoneechee Council

Servings: 10–12
Preparation Time: 1 hour
Challenge Level: Easy

Dandy Deviled Eggs

12 eggs

½ cup mayonnaise

½ cup sour cream

1 teaspoon white vinegar

¼ teaspoon celery salt

1 teaspoon powdered mustard

Ground paprika for garnish

PREPARATION AT CAMP:

1. Place eggs in cook pot and bring water to a full boil for about 1 minute (and no more).
2. Remove pot from heat and allow eggs to sit for about 30 minutes in the hot water.
3. Bathe eggs in cold water to cool them off.
4. Peel the eggs.
5. Slice each egg in half and carefully remove the yolk halves, placing the yolks in a heavy-duty gallon-size ziplock bag. Set egg whites on a serving tray or other clean surface.
6. Add mayonnaise, sour cream, vinegar, celery salt, and powdered mustard to the bag. Seal and mush ingredients together.
7. Cut a small corner from the bottom of the bag.
8. Using the bag like a cake decorator might, squeeze a generous amount of egg mixture into each egg hole.
9. Sprinkle eggs with paprika and serve.

REQUIRED EQUIPMENT:

Medium-size cook pot
1 (1-gallon) heavy-duty ziplock bag

Tim Conners, Statesboro, Georgia
Assistant Scoutmaster
Troop 340, Coastal Empire Council

Christine Conners, Statesboro, Georgia
Committee Member and Merit Badge Counselor
Troop 340, Coastal Empire Council

Servings: 12 (2 half-eggs per serving)
Preparation Time: 1 hour
Challenge Level: Moderate

Troop 49 Killer Dip

- 2 pounds ground sausage
- 2 (8-ounce) packages cream cheese
- 2 (10-ounce) cans Ro*Tel tomatoes
- 2 (12-ounce) bags tortilla chips

"I was given this recipe by a lady leader when I first joined Scouts and have been making it for the Troop and Order of the Arrow for over fifteen years now."

PREPARATION AT CAMP:

1. In a large skillet, brown the sausage.
2. Add cream cheese and Ro*Tel tomatoes then stir to blend.
3. Remove from heat and serve with chips.

REQUIRED EQUIPMENT:

Large frying pan

Beverly Jo Antonini, Morgantown, West Virginia
Assistant Scoutmaster
Troop 49, Mountaineer Area Council

Cooking corn for the troop. SCOTT H. SIMERLY SR.

Servings: 12–14
Preparation Time: ¼ hour
Challenge Level: Easy

BASR Steamed Broccoli

"This dish came about for two reasons. First, it is very easy to cook and adapt to your group size (we have prepared it for as many as 200 people). Second, kids generally like broccoli (cauliflower is not nearly as popular). We try to incorporate vegetables into our meals, and this one works. We remind the Scouts that we eat to go camping. We don't go camping to eat. The recipe is named for our favorite place to camp: Bert Adams Scout Reservation."

4 bunches broccoli, cut into pieces about 2 inches long

Italian seasoning and salt to taste

PREPARATION AT CAMP:

1. Put about an inch of water in large frying pan and set over medium-high heat.
2. Add broccoli to pan.
3. Cover with foil.
4. Bring to boil and steam for 15 to 30 minutes, until crunchy-tender. The broccoli can be turned, moving the top pieces to the bottom, after about 10 minutes.
5. Sprinkle with seasoning and serve.

REQUIRED EQUIPMENT:

Large frying pan
Aluminum foil (to fashion a lid)

Carl Wust Jr., Conyers, Georgia
Scoutmaster
Troop 410, Atlanta Area Council

Servings: 14–16
Preparation Time: ¾ hour
Challenge Level: Easy

Conestoga River Scalloped Potatoes

- 8 medium potatoes, peeled and thinly sliced
- 2 small onions, thinly sliced
- ⅔ cup all-purpose flour
- 2 teaspoons salt
- 1 teaspoon ground black pepper
- ½ cup (1 standard stick) butter, thinly sliced
- 4 cups milk
- 1 cup Progresso Italian Style Bread Crumbs

"This recipe requires some peeling and slicing of the potatoes and onions, which the new Scouts are always eager to do after achieving their Totin' Chip card and permission to use the knives."

PREPARATION AT CAMP:

1. Alternate layers of potatoes and onions in the Dutch oven.
2. Sprinkle each layer with flour, salt, black pepper, and slices of butter.
3. Once all ingredients are layered, pour milk over all.
4. Sprinkle bread crumbs over the top.
5. Bake for about 1 hour, using 22 coals on the lid and 12 briquettes under the oven, until the potatoes are tender. Refresh coals as required.

REQUIRED EQUIPMENT:

14-inch camp Dutch oven

James Landis, New Providence, Pennsylvania
Unit Commissioner
Conestoga River District, Pennsylvania Dutch Council

Servings: 14–16
Preparation Time: 1¼ hours
Challenge Level: Easy

Terminator Beans

1 pound bacon, chopped into pieces

1 pound lean ground beef

1 pound ground sausage

1 large red onion, chopped

⅔ cup granulated sugar

⅔ cup brown sugar

¼ cup molasses

½ cup barbecue sauce

½ cup ketchup

12 drops Tabasco sauce

2 tablespoons prepared mustard

2 teaspoons horseradish

1 teaspoon salt

1 teaspoon fresh ground black pepper

4 cloves garlic, minced

1 (20-ounce) can crushed pineapple and juice

2 (16-ounce) cans pork and beans

1 (16-ounce) can black-eyed peas, drained

1 (16-ounce) can kidney beans, drained

1 (16-ounce) can great northern beans, drained

1 (16-ounce) can pinto beans, drained

PREPARATION AT CAMP:

1. In Dutch oven preheated over 25 coals, brown bacon, ground beef, sausage, and onions until onions become translucent.
2. Drain fat from oven then add the remainder of ingredients and mix well.
3. Cook for 30 minutes with lid off, using only 12 coals underneath the oven, stirring occasionally.
4. Refresh coals, covering oven and cooking for an additional 30 minutes, using 17 coals on the lid and 8 briquettes under the oven.

REQUIRED EQUIPMENT:

12-inch camp Dutch oven

Shane Roe, Kearns, Utah
Assistant Scoutmaster
Troop 1769, Great Salt Lake Council

Servings: 18–20
Preparation Time: 1¾ hours
Challenge Level: Moderate

Bison Baked Beans

1 pound ground bison (venison or lean ground beef can be substituted)

1 cup chopped onion

2 (53¼-ounce) cans Campbell's Pork and Beans

2 cups brown sugar

1 (18-ounce) bottle KC Masterpiece Original barbecue sauce

Option: Cooking time can be shortened to as little as 1 hour, but the flavor of the sauce will not be as intense.

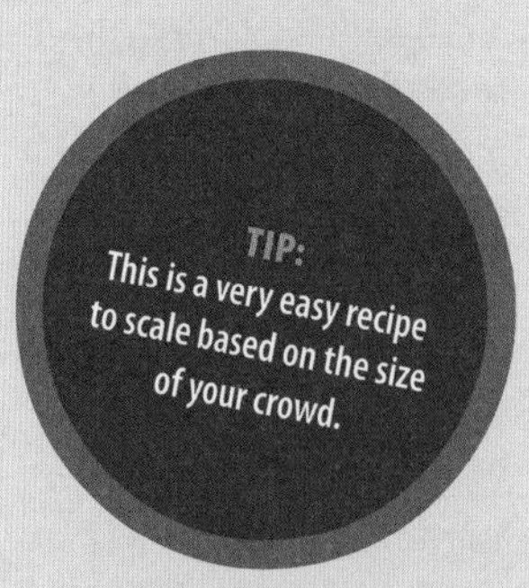

Servings: 18–20
Preparation Time: 2½ hours
Challenge Level: Easy

"The Scouts won't easily mess this recipe up, even if they are inaccurate on the ingredients. The boys can certainly burn the beans in the Dutch oven if they don't watch the heat. But other than that, they'll turn out pretty well regardless."

PREPARATION AT CAMP:

1. Over 25 coals, brown the meat and onions in Dutch oven.
2. Drain as much liquid from beans as possible to keep the dish from becoming runny.
3. Pour beans, brown sugar, and barbecue sauce into the oven. Stir until lumps of brown sugar have dissolved.
4. Move 15 coals to the lid and reduce coals to only 6 briquettes under the oven.
5. Bake for about 2 hours, refreshing coals as required and stirring beans every 20 minutes.

REQUIRED EQUIPMENT:
12-inch camp Dutch oven

Emery Corley, Saint Louis, Missouri
Assistant Scoutmaster
Troop 809, Greater Saint Louis Area Council

Waldorf Salad

"Waldorf salad was created in the 1890s by Oscar Tschirky, the maître d'hôtel of the Waldorf-Astoria hotel in Manhattan. The original recipe contained only apples, celery, and mayonnaise, but walnuts were soon added. This is an easy and flexible salad to prepare."

PREPARATION AT CAMP:

1. Chill all ingredients if they aren't already.
2. Wash, core, and chop apples into small pieces.
3. Toss apples with lemon juice in a large bowl to minimize browning.
4. Combine the remainder of ingredients, except for optional lettuce, with the apples in the bowl. Toss well.
5. Serve on an optional bed of lettuce.

REQUIRED EQUIPMENT:

Large mixing bowl

Ken Harbison, Rochester, New York
Former Boy Scout and Master Tester for *The Scout's Outdoor Cookbook*
Washington Trail Council

Servings			
8	**16**	**24**	**Ingredients**
4	8	12	crisp apples (Cortland, Fuji, Gala, Jonagold, Pink Lady, or Delicious work well)
2 teaspoons	4 teaspoons	2 tablespoons	lemon juice
2	4	6	stalks celery, diced
1 cup	2 cups	3 cups	seedless grapes, halved, or Mandarin oranges, drained
½ cup	1 cup	1½ cups	raisins or dried cranberries
1 cup	2 cups	3 cups	walnuts, coarsely chopped
1 cup	2 cups	3 cups	light mayonnaise, Miracle Whip, or plain yogurt
1 cup	2 cups	3 cups	mini marshmallows (optional)
1	1½	2	heads lettuce (optional)

Servings: 8–24
Preparation Time: ½ hour
Challenge Level: Easy

Fruit Kabobs

"It can be a challenge to get Scouts to eat their vegetables, but fruit is usually always popular, even more so on a warm day."

PREPARATION AT CAMP:

1. Clean and cut fruit as required.
2. Coat apples and bananas in lemon or lime juice in a large bowl to help preserve their color.
3. Add remainder of cut fruit to the large bowl and gently stir to mix the pieces.
4. With clean hands, thread individual pieces of fruit onto bamboo skewers.

REQUIRED EQUIPMENT:

Large mixing bowl
Bamboo skewers

TIP: The variations for this recipe are nearly limitless, especially when substituting ingredients for fruit in season.

Tim Conners, Statesboro, Georgia
Assistant Scoutmaster
Troop 340, Coastal Empire Council

Christine Conners, Statesboro, Georgia
Committee Member and Merit Badge Counselor
Troop 340, Coastal Empire Council

Servings			
8	**16**	**24**	**Ingredients**
1	2	3	20-ounce cans pineapple chunks, drained
1	2	3	small melons (honeydew, cantaloupe, or watermelon), seeded and cubed
1 pound	2 pounds	3 pounds	sliced strawberries
1 pound	2 pounds	3 pounds	green or red seedless grapes
2	4	6	tart apples, cored, peeled, and cubed
2	4	6	bananas, peeled and cut into ½-inch-thick slices
2	4	6	lemons or limes, juiced

Servings: 8–24
Preparation Time: ½ hour
Challenge Level: Moderate

Class-A Baked Potatoes

PREPARATION AT HOME:

1. Prepare dressing by combining all dressing ingredients in a medium-size container with lid, stirring gently with a whisk.
2. Keep cool until camp. Dressing can be refrigerated for up to 5 days.

PREPARATION AT CAMP:

1. Scrub potatoes and poke numerous deep holes into them with a fork.
2. Lightly grease the potatoes with vegetable oil then securely wrap each in heavy-duty aluminum foil.
3. Bury potatoes in the coals of the campfire.
4. Check potatoes by inserting a cooking fork every 10 minutes or so to check for doneness. The potatoes are ready when the fork goes deep into the potato easily.
5. While potatoes are cooking, break broccoli florets into small pieces.
6. In a medium-size cook pot, steam florets in about 1 to 2 cups of water. Broccoli will be ready when warmed through and still slightly crunchy.
7. When potatoes are finished cooking, cut open the potatoes and place about ¼ cup of broccoli into each potato.
8. Pour peppercorn ranch dressing over broccoli into potato and serve, reserving enough for each potato.

Servings		
12	**24**	**Dressing ingredients**
1½ cups	3 cups	buttermilk
½ cup	1 cup	sour cream
¼ cup	½ cup	mayonnaise
¼ cup	½ cup	grated Parmesan cheese
1 tablespoon	2 tablespoons	dried parsley
1 teaspoon	2 teaspoons	onion powder
½ teaspoon	1 teaspoon	dried oregano
½ teaspoon	1 teaspoon	garlic powder
½ teaspoon	1 teaspoon	salt
¼ teaspoon	½ teaspoon	coarse ground black pepper
		Other ingredients
12	24	medium baking potatoes
		vegetable oil for greasing potatoes
3 cups	6 cups	broccoli florets

REQUIRED EQUIPMENT:

Medium-size cook pot
Medium-size container with lid
Heavy-duty aluminum foil

Charles Flay, Yadkinville, North Carolina
Unit Commissioner
Pack 699, Old Hickory Council

Servings: 12–24
Preparation Time: ¾ hour
Challenge Level: Moderate

Power-Drill Garlic Mashed Potatoes

"This recipe is a favorite in my troop. With it, I have 'converted' all the Scouts who were very picky eaters into the kind who say, 'Could I have some more?' I actually use a battery-powered drill and a clean, heavy-duty paint stirrer to really fluff the potatoes up."

TIPS:

- The smaller the size of the potato cubes, the faster they will cook.
- Hand-whipping a large batch of potatoes is tedious work, requiring more than one set of hands for really large batches. If available, a powered mixer will make the job much easier and the potatoes even smoother.

PREPARATION AT CAMP:

1. Place potatoes in a large pot, and fill pot with just enough water to cover the potatoes.
2. Add half of the crushed garlic to the water in the pot.
3. Bring to a boil and cook until the potatoes are easily pierced with a fork. Cooking time can vary significantly depending on the cut-size and type of potatoes.
4. Carefully drain water from the pot.
5. Add butter to the potatoes and mash with potato masher until all the big clumps are gone and butter is melted.
6. Add heavy cream, sugar, steak or chicken seasoning, onion powder, garlic powder, and remaining crushed garlic. Whip with mixer until smooth.

Servings: 10–30
Preparation Time: 1 hour
Challenge Level: Moderate

REQUIRED EQUIPMENT:

Large cook pot (at least 10-quart size if cooking 24 servings)
Potato masher
Hand-mixer (battery-powered drill optional)

John Malachowski, Stewartstown, Pennsylvania
Scoutmaster
Troop 27, New Birth of Freedom Council

Servings			
10	**20**	**30**	**Ingredients**
5 pounds	10 pounds	15 pounds	medium red potatoes, washed and cut into ½- to 1-inch cubes
4 teaspoons	3 tablespoons	4 tablespoons	crushed garlic
1 cup	2 cups	3 cups	butter
½ cup	1 cup	1½ cups	heavy cream
2 teaspoons	4 teaspoons	2 tablespoons	sugar
1 teaspoon	2 teaspoons	1 tablespoons	steak or chicken seasoning (any brand)
¼ teaspoon	½ teaspoon	¾ teaspoon	onion powder
½ teaspoon	1 teaspoon	1½ teaspoons	garlic powder

Option: Amish butter is wonderful in this recipe.

Mountain Man Beans

PREPARATION AT CAMP:

1. In Dutch oven preheated over 32 coals, brown ground beef.
2. Add chopped bell peppers, onions, and Smokies. Sauté until onions become translucent.
3. Add pineapple, Italian sauce, pork and beans, and garlic salt. Stir.
4. Reduce coal-count under the oven to 25 briquettes and continue to cook, simmering the beans for at least ½ hour.

REQUIRED EQUIPMENT:

Deep 14-inch camp Dutch oven

Tim Ward, Pulaski, Virginia
Committee Member
Troop 48, Blue Ridge Mountains Council

Sautéing some sides on a Dutch oven lid!
SCOTT H. SIMERLY SR.

2 pounds lean ground beef

2 green bell peppers, chopped

1 yellow bell pepper, chopped

2 onions, chopped

3 (14-ounce) packs Lit'l Smokies links

1 (20-ounce) can crushed pineapple (do not drain)

1 (24-ounce) jar Prego Traditional Italian sauce

1 (117-ounce) can pork and beans

2 teaspoons garlic salt

Servings: 28–30
Preparation Time: 1¼ hours
Challenge Level: Easy

Campfire Cheesy Onion Bread

2 (1-pound) French loaves, cut lengthwise into top and bottom pieces

½ cup (1 standard stick) butter

24 slices American cheese (or your favorite)

1 medium white onion, thinly sliced

Option: For a sweeter taste, onions can be cooked in aluminum foil before placing on the loaf.

TIP:
To achieve more even baking results, a simple reflector oven can be constructed next to the fire by making a "lean-to" out of foil, with the open end toward the fire to reflect the heat toward the loaf inside.

"This recipe is a simple way to introduce Scouts to the concept of a reflector oven."

PREPARATION AT CAMP:

1. Place both halves of each loaf open-side up.
2. Spread a thin layer of butter on each of the halves.
3. Place 6 slices of American cheese along each bottom half.
4. Lay onions evenly over the cheese.
5. Place another 6 slices of cheese over the onions on each bottom half then place top half of each loaf over the bottom.
6. Completely and tightly wrap each loaf in foil.
7. Place loaves within 6 inches to the side of a hot fire, enough to absorb the heat but not enough to burn.
8. After about 3 minutes, turn each loaf so that the other side faces the fire.
9. Cook for an additional 3 minutes.
10. Remove loaves from the foil and slice into 2-inch sections. Serve.

REQUIRED EQUIPMENT:
Heavy-duty aluminum foil

Jason Cagle, Jacksonville, Florida
Assistant Scoutmaster
Troop 169, North Florida Council

Servings: 8–10
Preparation Time: ½ hour
Challenge Level: Easy

Great Rivers Date Bread

2 cups boiling water

1½ pounds chopped dates

2 teaspoons baking soda

2 cups granulated sugar

½ cup vegetable shortening

2 eggs

2 cups all-purpose flour

2 cups whole-wheat flour

1 cup chopped walnuts

PREPARATION AT CAMP:

1. In a small bowl, pour boiling water over dates and baking soda then set aside.
2. In a large bowl, whisk together sugar, shortening, and eggs until creamy.
3. Add flours and nuts to egg mixture, along with the dates, previously set aside, and mix well.
4. Spread date dough in the bottom of well-greased Dutch oven.
5. Bake for 1¼ hours, using 20 coals on the lid and 10 briquettes under the oven, until a knife comes out clean.

REQUIRED EQUIPMENT:

14-inch camp Dutch oven
Small mixing bowl
Large mixing bowl

Richard Parkhurst, Sedalia, Missouri
Council Member
Great Rivers Council

Servings: 12–14
Preparation Time: 1½ hours
Challenge Level: Easy

Sequoia Sweet Potato Biscuits

5 cups self-rising flour

1 cup light brown sugar

1½ teaspoons ground cinnamon

1 teaspoon ground ginger

½ teaspoon ground allspice

¾ cup vegetable shortening

1 (29-ounce) can cut sweet potatoes, drained

1 cup whipping cream

½ cup pecans, chopped fine

HONEY BUTTER TOPPING:

½ cup butter

½ cup honey

TIP:
5 cups of all-purpose flour along with 7 teaspoons baking powder and 2½ teaspoons salt can be substituted for the 5 cups of self-rising flour.

Servings: 16–18
Preparation Time: 1¼ hours
Challenge Level: Moderate

PREPARATION AT CAMP:

1. Line Dutch oven with heavy-duty aluminum foil and lightly grease the foil.
2. Mix together flour, brown sugar, cinnamon, ginger, and allspice in a large bowl.
3. Cut in the shortening.
4. Mash drained sweet potatoes with whipping cream in a medium-size bowl using a potato masher and add to flour-shortening mixture. Blend well.
5. Roll ⅓-cup portions of dough into balls and flatten slightly before placing in oven. Dough will be sticky. Distribute biscuit dough evenly in the oven.
6. Cover biscuit dough with chopped pecans.
7. Bake for about 40 minutes, using 22 coals on the lid and 12 briquettes under the oven, until golden brown.
8. While biscuits bake, mix butter and honey in small mixing bowl.
9. Serve hot biscuits with whipped honey butter.

REQUIRED EQUIPMENT:

14-inch camp Dutch oven
Large mixing bowl
Medium-size mixing bowl
Small mixing bowl
Potato masher
Heavy-duty aluminum foil

Mac McCoy, Hanford, California
Assistant District Commissioner
Sequoia Council

Scoutmaster's Corn Bread

8 (8½-ounce) boxes Jiffy Corn Muffin mix

8 eggs

2 cups milk

1 small onion, chopped

1 small bell pepper, chopped

2 (14¾-ounce) cans creamed corn

1 (2-ounce) package pre-cooked bacon, crumbled

2 teaspoons salt

2 teaspoons ground black pepper

½ cup granulated sugar

8 ounces (2 cups) grated cheese (your choice)

PREPARATION AT CAMP:

1. Mix all ingredients in a large bowl.
2. Let batter rest for a few minutes.
3. Line Dutch oven with heavy-duty aluminum foil and grease the foil.
4. Pour batter into oven.
5. Bake for about 1¼ hours, using 21 coals on the lid and 11 briquettes under the oven, until bread becomes golden and a toothpick comes out clean. Refresh coals as required.

REQUIRED EQUIPMENT:

14-inch camp Dutch oven
Large mixing bowl
Heavy-duty aluminum foil

Barry Moore, Tampa, Florida
Former District Chairman
Lake Region District, Gulf Ridge Council

Option: Goes great with Scoutmaster's Seafood Jambalaya, also in this book.

It's easy to bake awesome breads in a Dutch oven.

TIM CONNERS

Servings: 20–22
Preparation Time: 1½ hour
Challenge Level: Easy

Hazard Lake Zucchini Rolls

"I've prepared this dish in as many as five Dutch ovens at the same time, and there was never a crumb left over. This recipe is named for Hazard Lake in the Payette National Forest, near McCall, Idaho."

1 cup milk

½ cup shortening, reserving 1 tablespoon to sauté zucchini

1 cup grated green zucchini

½ cup granulated sugar

¾ teaspoon salt

4 cups all-purpose flour

1 (1¼-ounce) packet active dry yeast

½ cup warm water

4 tablespoons (½ standard stick) butter, melted

¼ cup grated Parmesan cheese

3 tablespoons sesame seeds

1 tablespoon dried parsley

REQUIRED EQUIPMENT:

2 12-inch camp Dutch ovens
Small saucepan
Small mixing bowl
Large mixing bowl

PREPARATION AT CAMP:

1. In small saucepan, heat milk to almost boiling.
2. Pour scalded milk into a small bowl then add shortening, reserving 1 tablespoon shortening for the next step.
3. Sauté grated zucchini in the small saucepan in the reserved shortening until zucchini turns a bright green.
4. Add zucchini to hot milk mixture in the bowl. Stir well, breaking up any clumps of shortening.
5. Combine sugar, salt, and flour in large mixing bowl.
6. Dissolve yeast in warm (not hot) water in a cup.
7. Let zucchini mixture cool to lukewarm then add warm yeast water. Stir.
8. Add zucchini mixture to dry ingredients in the large bowl and stir well. Knead, adding more flour if dough is runny, or water if dough is too dry.
9. Cover dough and let sit until doubled in volume.
10. Punch down dough, divide in half, then form each half into 15 rolls each.
11. Grease two Dutch ovens and place 15 rolls of dough into each oven, spacing the rolls evenly on the bottom.
12. Drizzle melted butter over both sets of rolls.
13. In small dish, combine Parmesan cheese, sesame seeds, and parsley. Sprinkle cheese-seed mixture over rolls in each Dutch oven.
14. Let rolls rise until doubled in volume once again.
15. Bake for about 30 minutes, using 17 coals on each lid and 8 briquettes under each oven, until the rolls become a light golden brown.

Servings: 30
Preparation Time: 3½ hours
Challenge Level: Difficult

David Wixom, New Plymouth, Idaho
Committee Member
Troop 386, Ore-Ida Council

TIP: If the water or zucchini mixture is too hot, it could kill the yeast and the rolls will turn out flat.

Chocoladas

1 (10½-ounce) bag mini marshmallows

4 (1.55-ounce) Hershey's milk chocolate bars

10 large flour tortillas

PREPARATION AT CAMP:

1. Spread about ⅓ cup marshmallows and 4 or 5 pieces of chocolate in each tortilla.
2. Fold like a burrito.
3. Wrap securely in foil, aligning the seam of the tortilla with the seam of the foil on top.
4. Cook for 5 to 10 minutes on a grill grate over low heat or flame.

REQUIRED EQUIPMENT:

Heavy-duty aluminum foil

Options:

Substitute butterscotch, white chocolate, or Heath chips for the milk chocolate.

Chocoladas can also be cooked in a skillet with butter, minus the foil of course.

Louis Hoffman, Minneapolis, Minnesota
Committee Chair
Troop 185, Northern Star Council

Servings: 10
Preparation Time: ¼ hour
Challenge Level: Easy

Mugs of Joy Banana Pudding

1 (5¼-ounce) package instant vanilla pudding

2 cups milk

1 (8-ounce) container sour cream

1 (14-ounce) can sweetened condensed milk

1 (12-ounce) box vanilla wafers

6 bananas, sliced

1 (12-ounce) container Cool Whip

PREPARATION AT CAMP:

1. In sealed gallon-size ziplock bag, mash pudding with milk until blended, following directions on pudding box regarding time required to set (thicken).
2. Once pudding has set, add sour cream and sweetened condensed milk to the ziplock bag. Seal and knead to blend.
3. Cut a small corner from the bottom of the bag for neatly squeezing pudding into mugs.
4. In each of 12 mugs or cups, layer pudding first, followed by vanilla wafers, then sliced bananas, and finally Cool Whip.

REQUIRED EQUIPMENT:
Gallon-size heavy-duty ziplock bag

Jason Cagle, Jacksonville, Florida
Assistant Scoutmaster
Troop 169, North Florida Council

Sticky buns and monkey breads make great dessert options. *SCOTT H. SIMERLY SR.*

Servings: 12
Preparation Time: ¼ hour
Challenge Level: Easy

Webelos Hot Banana Splits

12 fresh bananas, peeled

1 (11¾-ounce) jar Smucker's pineapple topping

1 (11¾-ounce) jar Smucker's strawberry topping

1 (11¾-ounce) jar Smucker's chocolate fudge topping

1 (10½-ounce) bag mini marshmallows

1 (2¼-ounce) bag chopped peanuts

1 (15-ounce) can Reddi-wip

PREPARATION AT CAMP:

1. Cut aluminum foil into twelve 12 x 12-inch sheets.
2. Cut each peeled banana lengthwise, tip to tip, ¾ of the way deep.
3. Carefully open banana and place one on each foil sheet.
4. Spread 1 heaping tablespoon each of pineapple, strawberry, and fudge toppings on each banana.
5. Cover each banana with marshmallows and sprinkle with nuts.
6. Bring sides of foil up around each banana split and close top and sides by folding edges over, creating an airtight seal. If the banana splits have been customized, use a permanent marker to write names on the foil at this time.
7. Place each foil pack on grill over medium heat for about 10 to 15 minutes.
8. Remove with tongs and carefully open from the top, being careful to avoid escaping steam.
9. Serve in the foil or on a plate with a spoon, topping with Reddi-wip.

REQUIRED EQUIPMENT:

Standard size heavy-duty aluminum foil

Bruce Faber, Antioch, Illinois
Webelos Den Leader
Pack 190, Northeast Illinois Council

Servings: 12
Preparation Time: ½ hour
Challenge Level: Easy

Belgian Pumpkin Torte

"This recipe won the Silver Spatula award at the 2009 Tidelands District Cubmaster Cook-Off."

1 (18¼-ounce) box yellow cake mix

1 egg plus 2 eggs

½ cup vegetable oil

1 (15-ounce) can pure pumpkin

1 (12-ounce) can evaporated milk

2 teaspoons pumpkin pie spice

½ teaspoon salt

½ cup granulated sugar

3 tablespoons butter

¼ cup chopped pecans

1 (14-ounce) can Reddi-wip

PREPARATION AT CAMP:

1. Set aside 1 cup cake mix. Combine remaining cake mix, 1 egg, and vegetable oil in a medium-size bowl. Stir well.
2. Spread and flatten cake batter in greased Dutch oven.
3. In another medium-size bowl, combine 2 eggs, pumpkin, evaporated milk, pumpkin pie spice, and salt.
4. Stir well then pour pumpkin mixture over cake batter in oven.
5. In a small bowl, mix 1 cup of cake mix, previously set aside, with sugar and butter.
6. Sprinkle cake mix-butter crumbles over pumpkin filling in oven.
7. Top all with chopped nuts.
8. Bake for 1 hour, using 17 coals on the lid and 8 briquettes under the oven. Refresh coals as required.
9. Serve with Reddi-wip.

REQUIRED EQUIPMENT:

12-inch camp Dutch oven
2 medium-size mixing bowls
Small mixing bowl

Jimmy Hancock, Savannah, Georgia
Eagle Scout and Cubmaster
Pack 11, Coastal Empire Council

Servings: 12–14
Preparation Time: 1½ hours
Challenge Level: Easy

Black Creek Boiled Peanuts

"Unheard of most everywhere else, boiled peanuts are a huge hit in the South. They deserve broader recognition, because they are easy to prepare, wholesome, and the Scouts love them. We named this recipe after the Coastal Empire's new council camp."

5 pounds raw green peanuts in the shell

1 cup salt

Water, enough to cover peanuts

Option: For Cajun-like flair, substitute Old Bay seasoning to taste for the salt.

PREPARATION AT CAMP:

1. Pour peanuts and salt into a large pot with strainer basket.
2. Add enough water to cover peanuts.
3. Over medium-high heat, cover and boil for approximately 3 hours, until the shells of the peanuts become soft. Add more water as required to keep peanuts covered.
4. Drain and serve.

REQUIRED EQUIPMENT:

Large cook pot with strainer basket

Tim Conners, Statesboro, Georgia
Assistant Scoutmaster
Troop 340, Coastal Empire Council

Christine Conners, Statesboro, Georgia
Committee Member and Merit Badge Counselor
Troop 340, Coastal Empire Council

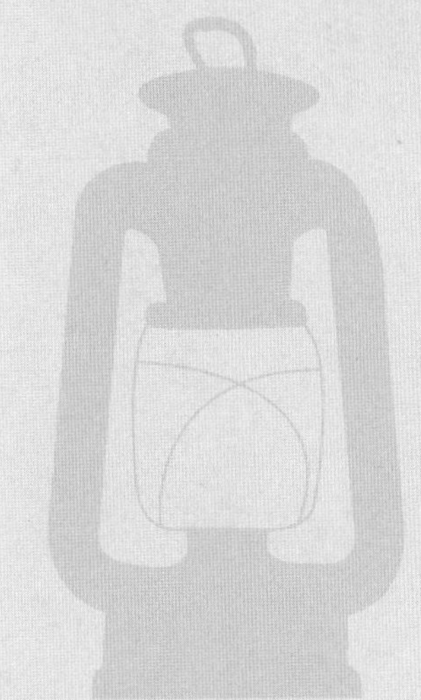

Servings: 12–14
Preparation Time: 3 hours
Challenge Level: Easy

Hands-On Apple Crisp

2¼ cups all-purpose flour

2¼ cups brown sugar

1½ cups old-fashioned oats

4½ teaspoons ground cinnamon

1 tablespoon apple pie spice

1½ cups (3 standard sticks) butter, softened

12 large Granny Smith apples, cored and sliced

"This is a great hands-on recipe that is easy to prepare in camp. The first people in line take only a small amount to be polite, but it still always seems to run out before everyone gets some. The ones who go hungry are then first in line the next time. They don't want to miss out twice in a row. You will not believe the great aroma . . . it's as good as Grandma's."

PREPARATION AT HOME:

1. Combine flour, brown sugar, oats, cinnamon, and apple pie spice in a gallon-size heavy-duty ziplock bag.
2. Pack flour mixture for camp.

PREPARATION AT CAMP:

1. Add butter to ziplock bag filled with dry ingredients. Seal bag and thoroughly mush ingredients together with hands.
2. Spread sliced apples evenly in Dutch oven.
3. Spoon butter-flour mixture evenly over the apples.
4. Bake for 1 hour, using 21 coals on the lid and 11 briquettes under the oven. Refresh coals as required.

REQUIRED EQUIPMENT:

14-inch camp Dutch oven
Gallon-size heavy-duty ziplock bag

Patrick Jarboe, Battle Ground, Indiana
Den Leader
Pack 3311, Sagamore Council

Servings: 14–16
Preparation Time: 1¼ hours
Challenge Level: Easy

Death by Chocolate

"This recipe has not won awards yet, but I have had several Scouts and adults tell me it should have."

½ cup vegetable oil

½ cup cocoa powder

1 cup brown sugar

1½ cups water

1 (10½-ounce) bag mini marshmallows

FOR CAKE BATTER:

1 (18¼-ounce) box Betty Crocker SuperMoist Chocolate Fudge cake mix

1⅓ cups water

½ cup vegetable oil

3 eggs

1 cup chocolate chips

1 (12-ounce) container Cool Whip

PREPARATION AT CAMP:

1. Combine ½ cup vegetable oil, cocoa powder, brown sugar, and 1½ cups water in a medium-size bowl. Mix well.
2. Pour cocoa-oil mixture in foil-lined Dutch oven.
3. Add mini marshmallows to top of cocoa mixture.
4. Prepare cake batter by blending cake mix, 1⅓ cups water, ½ cup vegetable oil, and eggs in mixing bowl.
5. Pour cake mix on top of marshmallows.
6. Sprinkle chocolate chips on top of cake batter.
7. Bake for 1 hour, using 17 coals on the lid and 8 briquettes under the oven. Refresh coals as required.
8. Serve warm and top with Cool Whip.

REQUIRED EQUIPMENT:

12-inch camp Dutch oven
Medium-size mixing bowl
Heavy-duty aluminum foil

Tom Schneider, Cincinnati, Ohio
Committee Member
Troop 420, Dan Beard Council

Servings: 14–16
Preparation Time: 1¼ hours
Challenge Level: Easy

Strawberry Shortcake Cobbler

¼ cup (½ standard stick) butter

2 (21-ounce) cans strawberry pie filling

2 (18¼-ounce) packages Duncan Hines Strawberry Supreme cake mix

1 (12-ounce) can lemon-lime soda

PREPARATION AT CAMP:

1. Preheat Dutch oven over 8 coals.
2. Place about ⅓ of butter in oven to melt.
3. Pour strawberry filling into oven. Smooth out over the bottom.
4. Pour cake mix over the pie filling. Gently even out the cake mix without disturbing the pie filling underneath.
5. Slice the remaining butter and evenly distribute the pats over the cake mix.
6. Pour soda evenly over the cake mix. Do not stir.
7. Bake for 45 minutes, using 17 coals on the lid and 8 briquettes under the oven. Refresh coals if required.

REQUIRED EQUIPMENT:

12-inch camp Dutch oven

Dwight Bost, Melbourne, Florida
Committee Member
Troop 285, Central Florida Council

Servings: 14–16
Preparation Time: 1¼ hours
Challenge Level: Easy

Occoneechee Lemon Cornmeal Pie

1 cup (2 standard sticks) butter, softened

2 cups granulated sugar

1 tablespoon lemon extract

4 large eggs

1 cup cornmeal

2 (9-inch) frozen pie crusts in pans, thawed

PREPARATION AT CAMP:

1. Cream together butter, sugar, and lemon extract in a large bowl.
2. Stir eggs and cornmeal into the butter-sugar mixture then beat for about 5 minutes until well blended.
3. Divide batter between the pie shells.
4. Place a pie pan on a trivet in each of two Dutch ovens.
5. Bake for about 40 minutes, using 17 coals on the lid and 8 briquettes under the oven, until tops of pies become a golden brown.

REQUIRED EQUIPMENT:

2 12-inch camp Dutch ovens with trivets
Large mixing bowl

Scott Simerly, Apex, North Carolina
Scoutmaster
Troop 204, Occoneechee Council

Servings: 16
Preparation Time: 1 hour
Challenge Level: Easy

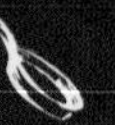

Court of Honor Peanut Butter Fudge

FUDGE:
1 cup (2 standard sticks) salted butter

1 cup creamy or crunchy peanut butter

1 pound confectioners' sugar

TOPPING:
1 (2.6-ounce) Hershey's chocolate bar

⅓ cup creamy peanut butter

"For family gatherings, my Aunt Betty would bring her famous Peanut Butter Fudge. Of all of the desserts on the table, it would always be the first to go, no matter how much she made. I was trusted to carry on the family recipe and was given a personal OK to share it before she passed away. I have made it for Courts of Honors, and of everything on the dessert table, it is still the first to run out."

PREPARATION AT CAMP:

1. To prepare fudge, melt butter over low heat in a medium-size pan.
2. Add 1 cup peanut butter and the confectioners' sugar. Mix well. Remove from heat.
3. Pat the fudge mixture evenly in an 8 x 8-inch baking pan.
4. To prepare topping, melt chocolate bar in a small pan over low heat, making certain not to burn the chocolate.
5. Mix in ⅓ cup peanut butter. Remove from heat.
6. Spread topping evenly over fudge.
7. Cover with plastic wrap or foil and place in cooler for about 1 hour to set.
8. Cut into 2 x 2-inch squares and serve.

REQUIRED EQUIPMENT:
Medium-size frying pan
Small frying pan
8 x 8-inch baking pan
Aluminum foil or plastic wrap

Jason Cagle, Jacksonville, Florida
Assistant Scoutmaster
Troop 169, North Florida Council

Servings: 16
Preparation Time: 1½ hours
Challenge Level: Easy

Campout Pudding Parfaits

"This recipe has been one of our most popular campout desserts with both Scouts and adults."

2 (5.9-ounce) boxes Jell-O instant chocolate pudding

6 cups milk

1 (12-ounce) box mini vanilla wafers

1 (1-pound) bag M&Ms

1 (14-ounce) can whipped cream

Candy dessert sprinkles

PREPARATION AT CAMP:

1. Combine chocolate pudding mix and milk in a gallon-size heavy-duty ziplock bag.
2. Securely seal the bag, knead pudding mixture well, and place over ice in cooler for about ½ hour to set.
3. Snip corner from bottom of bag for neatly squeezing pudding in the next step.
4. In mugs or cups, alternate layers of pudding, wafers, and M&Ms. Do this step just prior to serving so that the wafers stay crisp.
5. Top with whipped cream and sprinkles.

REQUIRED EQUIPMENT:
Gallon-size heavy-duty ziplock bag

Emery Corley, Saint Louis, Missouri
Assistant Scoutmaster
Troop 809, Greater Saint Louis Area Council

These desserts were obviously popular with the troop! *TRACY TUTTLE*

Servings: 16–18
Preparation Time: ¾ hour
Challenge Level: Easy

Hot Chocolate Cobbler

1½ cups (3 standard sticks) butter

3 cups self-rising flour

3 cups plus 1½ cups granulated sugar

1 tablespoon vanilla extract

1½ cups milk

1 cup cocoa powder

3 cups water

"Last fall, our troop went on a Camp-O-Ree, and when we arrived, we learned that the camp ranger had declared a total burn ban. We could not even use charcoal to cook with our Dutch ovens. So I had the boys split this recipe into two 8 x 8-inch square pans, and we cooked them in a stove-top oven, one at a time. We were the only troop to have dessert that night."

PREPARATION AT CAMP:

1. Melt butter in Dutch oven over 8 coals.
2. In a large bowl, mix flour, 3 cups sugar, vanilla extract, and milk.
3. Pour batter over melted butter.
4. Mix cocoa powder and 1½ cups sugar together in a small bowl.
5. Sprinkle cocoa mixture over the batter.
6. Slowly pour water evenly over the cocoa mixture. Do not stir.
7. Bake for about 45 minutes, using 17 coals on the lid and 8 briquettes under the oven, until batter sets. Refresh coals if required.

REQUIRED EQUIPMENT:

12-inch camp Dutch oven
Large mixing bowl
Small mixing bowl

Kenneth Scott Ford, Cabot, Arkansas
Eagle Scout and Committee Member
Troop 23, Quapaw Area Council

Servings: 18–20
Preparation Time: 1¼ hours
Challenge Level: Easy

Camp Chickagami Pineapple Upside-Down Pound Cake

"I was Scoutmaster of Troop 64 and had cemented a reputation for Dutch oven cooking. I had always hoped my legacy would be the number of Scouts I'd helped to the rank of Eagle, but what they remember most are my desserts.."

1 (20-ounce) can sliced pineapples, with juice

1 (10-ounce) jar maraschino cherries

½ cup brown sugar

6 eggs

1 cup vegetable oil

1 (20-ounce) can crushed pineapples, with juice

2 (18¼-ounce) boxes yellow cake mix

1 (8½-ounce) box Jiffy Corn Muffin mix

Water for batter, if needed

PREPARATION AT CAMP:

1. Line Dutch oven with foil. Grease foil and evenly arrange pineapple slices in bottom of the oven. Reserve pineapple juice for a later step.
2. Place about three maraschino cherries in the middle of each pineapple slice.
3. Take the juice drained from the pineapple slices and mix about half of it in a cup with brown sugar.
4. Drizzle sugar-juice syrup over pineapple slices.
5. In large mixing bowl, whisk eggs and oil.
6. Add crushed pineapple with juice, remaining cherries, and remaining juices from sliced pineapples and maraschino cherry jar to the egg-oil mixture.
7. Next, add cake mix and muffin mix to the large bowl. Stir well. If mix is too stiff, add only enough water to produce a thick batter.
8. Pour the batter over the sliced pineapples in the oven.
9. Bake for about 1 hour, using 20 coals on the lid and 10 briquettes under the oven, until a knife comes out clean. Refresh coals as needed. With this much sugar and size, it's easy to burn the cake; so get the coal count right and don't rush it.

REQUIRED EQUIPMENT:

14-inch camp Dutch oven
Large mixing bowl
Heavy-duty aluminum foil

Brent Roebuck, Painesville, Ohio
District Commissioner
Grand River District, Greater Western Reserve Council

Servings: 18–20
Preparation Time: 1½ hours
Challenge Level: Moderate

Cheesecake on a Shingle

"Had a craving for cheesecake one night and didn't want to go through the hassle of a difficult recipe. I looked through the kitchen and experimented with a few ingredients, and came up with a decent substitute. This is a good and easy treat for a Cracker Barrel."

PREPARATION AT CAMP:

1. Blend whipped cream cheese, vanilla extract, sugar, and lemon juice in medium-size bowl.
2. Evenly spread cream cheese mixture over graham crackers.
3. Top with optional strawberry jam.

REQUIRED EQUIPMENT:

Medium-size mixing bowl

Jason Cagle, Jacksonville, Florida
Assistant Scoutmaster
Troop 169, North Florida Council

Servings			
8	**16**	**24**	**Ingredients**
8 ounces	16 ounces	24 ounces	cream cheese, whipped
½ teaspoon	1 teaspoon	1½ teaspoons	vanilla extract
⅓ cup	⅔ cup	1 cup	granulated sugar
1 tablespoon	2 tablespoons	3 tablespoons	lemon juice
8	16	24	whole Honey Maid graham crackers
1	1	1	jar strawberry jam (optional)

Servings: 8–24
Preparation Time: ¼ hour
Challenge Level: Easy

Trapper Trails Rice Pudding

"This is delicious comfort food for Scouts away from home."

PREPARATION AT CAMP:

1. Combine all ingredients, except vanilla extract, in large pot.
2. Cook and stir until the mixture comes to a boil. Immediately remove from heat.
3. Cool for about 5 minutes, stirring once or twice.
4. Add vanilla extract, stir, and serve.

REQUIRED EQUIPMENT:

Large cook pot with heavy bottom

Sandra Dopp, Richmond, Utah
Roundtable Staff
Trapper Trails Council

Servings			
8	16	24	Ingredients
⅔ cup	1⅓ cups	2 cups	dry minute rice
¼ teaspoon	½ teaspoon	¾ teaspoon	salt
1	2	3	3-ounce packages Cook & Serve Jell-O Pudding and Pie Filling, coconut cream flavored
1 quart	2 quarts	3 quarts	milk
⅓ cup	⅔ cup	1 cup	granulated sugar
1	2	3	eggs, well beaten
¼ teaspoon	½ teaspoon	¾ teaspoon	ground cinnamon
⅛ teaspoon	¼ teaspoon	⅜ teaspoon	ground nutmeg
¼ cup	½ cup	¾ cup	raisins (optional)
¼ teaspoon	½ teaspoon	¾ teaspoon	vanilla extract

Servings: 8–24
Preparation Time: ½ hour
Challenge Level: Easy

Stove-Top Blueberry Pie

"This recipe comes from Scouter Brian Langley, owner-chef at The Lobster Pot restaurant in Ellsworth, Maine. In addition to being a restaurateur, Brian taught culinary arts in the school system. He is also our troop's Charter Rep. A few years ago, Brian taught the cooking merit badge to some of the boys in our troop. I don't know how much they retained, but I sure learned a lot. And I saved some of his recipes, including this one."

PREPARATION AT CAMP:

1. In a large cook pot with a heavy bottom, whisk together the cornstarch, salt, and about a third of the water to make a loose paste.
2. Add about a quarter of the blueberries, all the sugar, and the remaining water. Bring to a boil.
3. Reduce heat to medium and cook until the berry sauce thickens, stirring constantly.
4. Remove from heat and stir in lemon juice, cinnamon, and remaining blueberries.
5. Divide blueberry filling among pie shells and cool before serving.

REQUIRED EQUIPMENT:

Large cook pot with heavy bottom

Jim "Cinnamonboy" Rausch, Ellsworth, Maine
Assistant Scoutmaster
Troop 86, Katahdin Area Council

Servings			
8	**16**	**24**	**Ingredients**
¼ cup	½ cup	¾ cup	cornstarch
1	2	3	pinches salt
¾ cup	1½ cups	2¼ cups	water
4 cups	8 cups	12 cups	fresh blueberries
¾ cup	1½ cups	2¼ cups	granulated sugar
½ teaspoon	1 teaspoon	1½ teaspoons	lemon juice
1 teaspoon	2 teaspoons	1 tablespoon	ground cinnamon
1	2	3	9-inch precooked shortbread pie shells

Servings: 8–24
Preparation Time: 1 hour
Challenge Level: Easy

T-27's Wood Badge Sticky Buns

1 cup (2 standard sticks) butter

2 cups brown sugar

½ cup King Syrup (or corn syrup)

¼ cup ground cinnamon

3 tablespoons vanilla extract

1 (4.6-ounce) package Jell-O Cook & Serve vanilla pudding

Optional: 1 cup pecan pieces

1 (3-pound, 24-count) bag Rhodes frozen dinner rolls (or similar), thawed

Cooking spray

PREPARATION AT CAMP:

1. In a skillet over low heat, combine butter, brown sugar, syrup, cinnamon, vanilla extract, pudding mix, and optional pecans. Gently stir until butter melts and brown sugar dissolves.
2. Pour topping into foil-lined Dutch oven.
3. Lay dinner rolls side by side over topping.
4. Lightly coat top of dinner rolls with cooking spray. Cover rolls with plastic wrap.
5. Place lid over Dutch oven and allow dough to rise 6 to 8 hours.
6. Remove plastic wrap. (Don't forget this step; otherwise, the buns will end up covered with melted plastic.)
7. Lightly tap down on the rolls.
8. Bake for about 30 minutes, using 22 coals on the lid and 12 briquettes under the oven, until the tops of the rolls are light brown and an inserted knife comes out clean. Remove from heat.
9. Remove lid and place a large serving plate or pizza tray upside down over top of oven then carefully turn the plate and the oven over together. The buns will fall onto the plate. Remove foil and serve.

Caution: When flipping the oven on the last step, ask for assistance and wear protective gloves. Both the oven and caramel will be very hot.

REQUIRED EQUIPMENT:

14-inch camp Dutch oven
Medium-size frying pan
Heavy-duty aluminum foil
Plastic wrap

TIPS:

- Allow dough to rise overnight, and you'll be ready to bake sticky buns first thing in the morning.
- If the weather is cold, briefly heat the Dutch oven prior to assembling everything. After the oven is warmed to about 80°F, remove from coals or flame and quickly assemble the buns, then completely wrap the covered oven in a blanket to insulate it and keep it warm.

John Malachowski, Stewartstown, Pennsylvania
Scoutmaster
Troop 27, New Birth of Freedom Council

Servings: 24
Preparation Time: 1 hour (plus 6–8 hours rise time)
Challenge Level: Moderate

Sagamore Peach Cobbler

3 (18¼-ounce) boxes yellow cake mix

3 (29-ounce) cans peaches, drained

3 (12-ounce) cans lemon-lime soda

PREPARATION AT CAMP:

1. Pour dry cake mix into Dutch oven.
2. Spread peaches over top of cake mix.
3. Pour soda over all. Do not stir.
4. Bake for about 1 hour, using 21 coals on the lid and 11 briquettes under the oven, until the top becomes a golden brown.

REQUIRED EQUIPMENT:

14-inch camp Dutch oven

Janice Maynard, Sweetser, Indiana
Committee Member
Troop 433, Sagamore Council

Stove-top blueberry pie . . . oh yeah! *CHRISTINE CONNERS*

Servings: 24–26
Preparation Time: 1¼ hours
Challenge Level: Easy

Buckeyes

PREPARATION AT CAMP:

1. Pour oil in shallow pot and heat over medium flame.
2. Mix hot cocoa and sugar for coating in a gallon-size ziplock bag.
3. Coat each biscuit individually with cocoa-sugar mixture in the bag.
4. Fold dough to work the cocoa-sugar into each biscuit.
5. Repeat coating and folding process once again to produce more cocoa marbling.
6. Cut each marbled biscuit in half and roll into small balls ("buckeyes").
7. Carefully place the balls into the hot oil. They should sink initially then float as they cook.
8. Using tongs, flip the balls once the bottoms become golden brown.
9. Remove balls once they are uniformly golden and place on a paper towel to drain. Reduce flame temperature if the oil begins to smoke or if the outside of the buckeyes brown too quickly.
10. In sealed quart-size ziplock bag, knead all frosting ingredients, starting with a small amount of water. Continue to add water in very small quantities, if necessary, until the mixture is smooth.
11. Cut a small corner from the bottom of the bag and squirt frosting on the warm buckeyes.

REQUIRED EQUIPMENT:

Shallow medium-size cook pot
Gallon-size heavy-duty ziplock bag
Quart-size heavy-duty ziplock bag

Rick Pickelhaupt, East Amherst, New York
Eagle Scout and Scoutmaster
Troop 457, Greater Niagara Frontier Council

Servings: 10–30
Preparation Time: ¾ hour
Challenge Level: Moderate

Servings			
10	**20**	**30**	**Ingredients**
4 cups	4 cups	4 cups	vegetable oil (replenish oil as required for larger number of servings)
1	2	3	1-ounce packets hot cocoa mix
1 tablespoon	2 tablespoons	3 tablespoons	granulated sugar for coating
1	2	3	7½-ounce, 10-count containers refrigerated biscuit dough
Frosting:			
2 tablespoons	4 tablespoons	6 tablespoons	peanut butter (your favorite)
2 tablespoons	4 tablespoons	6 tablespoons	butter, softened
1 teaspoon	2 teaspoons	1 tablespoon	granulated sugar for frosting
1–2 teaspoons	3–4 teaspoons	4–5 teaspoons	water

Crew's 'Clairs

About 1 quart vegetable oil, depending on size of the skillet

3 (7½-ounce, 10-count) containers refrigerated Pillsbury buttermilk biscuits

4 (1.55-ounce) Hershey milk chocolate bars

1 (10½-ounce) bag mini marshmallows

Optional fillers: blueberries, raspberries, strawberries, or pie fillings

1 (24-ounce) container chocolate syrup

TIP:
Carefully control the heat. If the oil becomes too hot, the 'Clairs will brown on the outside before they fully cook on the inside. If the oil is not hot enough, the 'Clairs will end up soggy.

"Our crew became tired of s'mores and wanted something more 'adult.' That's how Crew's 'Clairs were born. They have been a huge hit wherever we go. The recipe takes a little patience to master, but it's well worth the effort. Make twice as many as you think you'll need. They're so good, people will demand seconds."

PREPARATION AT CAMP:

1. Pour oil into skillet to a depth of about 1 inch. Warm oil over medium heat.
2. Flatten each biscuit slightly and place 1 or 2 pieces of chocolate and 2 mini marshmallows in the center of the dough. Add any optional fillers at this time.
3. Fold dough over, trapping the chocolate and marshmallows in the pocket, and securely pinch the edges together.
4. Fry in oil until golden brown, turning once.
5. Serve, drizzling chocolate syrup over 'Clairs.

REQUIRED EQUIPMENT:

Large frying pan

Katherine Bleau, Thorndike, Massachusetts
Associate Adviser
Crew 164, Western Massachusetts Council

Servings: 30
Preparation Time: ½ hour
Challenge Level: Moderate

Mississippi Delta Pickles

"This recipe comes from the Mississippi Delta, where Scouts chomp on these things like candy."

1 gallon jar dill pickle spears

3 cups granulated sugar

6 cups water

6 (0.2-ounce) packages cherry, strawberry, or tropical punch unsweetened Kool-Aid mix

PREPARATION AT CAMP:

1. Remove pickles from the jar and discard pickle juice.
2. Mix sugar, water, and Kool-Aid in empty pickle jar.
3. Return pickles to the jar then marinate in a cooler for 2 to 3 days.

REQUIRED EQUIPMENT:

None

Richard Wallace, Bay City, Michigan
Adviser
Venture Crew 7100, Lake Huron Area Council

TIP:
The time to fully marinate the pickles takes days, so prepare at home in advance for shorter camping trips.

Servings: 40 (about 2 spears each)
Preparation Time: ¼ hour (plus 2–3 days for marinating)
Challenge Level: Easy

Yorktown Chocolate Chip Cookies

- 112 pounds chocolate chips
- 165 pounds all-purpose flour
- 500 eggs
- 100 pounds granulated sugar
- 87 pounds shortening
- 75 pounds brown sugar
- 12 pounds butter, softened
- 3 pounds salt
- 3 cups vanilla extract
- 1 quart water
- 1½ pounds baking soda

"When cooking for large groups, perhaps nothing trumps what it takes to prepare meals for the thousands of crewmembers aboard an aircraft carrier, a veritable floating city. The USS *Yorktown*, grande dame of the Pacific Theater in World War II, is now permanently anchored in Charleston Harbor. Nearly every Scout in the Southeast United States has made the pilgrimage at one time or other to tour this beloved carrier. It's basically a rite of passage. While the *Yorktown* is a very popular destination, what is less well known is the kitchen, found in the bowels of the ship, that was dedicated to baking 10,000 chocolate chip cookies every single day while at sea. It's a fascinating place to visit; and on the wall at the entry to the kitchen can be found the ingredients list, shown here. Even more remarkable is that the recipe actually scales very well, whether cooking for 10 or 10,000. Give it a try for your troop, and relive a little history."

PREPARATION AT CAMP:

1. Preheat greased Dutch oven, using 27 coals on the lid and 14 briquettes under the oven.
2. Scale ingredients for your group size. (Bring your calculator and use this book's conversion chart.)
3. Combine all ingredients in a large bowl. Mix well.
4. Roll spoon-size dollops of cookie dough into spheres and distribute in Dutch oven, leaving room for the dough from each cookie to melt and expand.
5. Bake for about 10 minutes, being careful to avoid burning bottom of cookies. Cook in batches as required for your group size.

REQUIRED EQUIPMENT:

16-inch camp Dutch oven
Large mixing bowl

USS *Yorktown*, Charleston, South Carolina
Low Country District, Coastal Carolina Council

TIP: Different size Dutch ovens can be accommodated with this recipe. Adjust the coal count to achieve a 375°F baking temperature for your equipment.

Servings: 10,000 (you may want to consider scaling for your particular group size)

Preparation Time: all day, every day (on a carrier) or ½ hour (at camp)

Challenge Level: Insane (on a carrier) or Easy (at camp)

Cowboy Coffee

"Our friend and former Scouter, Pete Fish, taught us how to make cowboy coffee on the trail. We've dabbled with his original recipe over the years to adapt it to camp and to larger groups. We've found cowboy coffee to be remarkably resilient against variations in cooking. Even when it's overboiled, it's still pretty darn good. Once, we inadvertently left an open pot of coffee over a low, smoky campfire for about half an hour. It was still at a moderate boil when we rediscovered it. Figuring it would be a bitter mess, instead, it was the best camp coffee we've ever tasted: smooth and mellow, presumably from the smoke."

1 cup coffee grounds, medium grind

3 quarts cold water

PREPARATION AT CAMP:

1. Over cold water in a pot, float coffee grounds to form a thick mat.
2. Bring water to a boil momentarily then remove from heat.
3. Add a splash of cold water to settle any grounds that remain floating on the surface.
4. Carefully scoop coffee from the top of liquid to avoid disturbing the settled grounds, unless you like the coffee chewy.

TIP:
Experiment with different grinds, roasts, strengths, and boiling times to find your perfect cup of camp coffee. And don't forget to try a little mellowing in the campfire smoke.

REQUIRED EQUIPMENT:
Medium-size cook pot

Tim Conners, Statesboro, Georgia
Assistant Scoutmaster
Troop 340, Coastal Empire Council

Christine Conners, Statesboro, Georgia
Committee Member and Merit Badge Counselor
Troop 340, Coastal Empire Council

Servings: 12 (about 6 ounces each)
Preparation Time: ¼ hour
Challenge Level: Easy

Hawaiian Spice Punch

2 (2-liter) bottles ginger ale, chilled

1 (12-ounce) container concentrated frozen pineapple juice

Optional: 2 oranges, sliced and cut into half-rounds

PREPARATION AT CAMP:

1. In a large punch bowl or container, combine ginger ale and pineapple juice concentrate.
2. Serve with optional orange half-rounds.

REQUIRED EQUIPMENT:

Large punch bowl or container with at least 5-quart capacity

Tim Conners, Statesboro, Georgia
Assistant Scoutmaster
Troop 340, Coastal Empire Council

Christine Conners, Statesboro, Georgia
Committee Member and Merit Badge Counselor
Troop 340, Coastal Empire Council

"Why do we always get stuck with the hot stove jobs and the other guys get to make punch?"

SCOTT H. SIMERLY SR.

Servings: 18 (about 8 ounces each)
Preparation Time: ¼ hour
Challenge Level: Easy

Mama Antonini's Hot Chocolate

"My mom used to prepare this recipe for my family long ago. Now, when my troop is camping out in the cold, I warm them up with the same hot chocolate treat."

2½ cups granulated sugar

1¼ cups Hershey's cocoa powder

1 teaspoon salt

2 teaspoons ground cinnamon

6⅔ cups Nido powdered milk mix

2 tablespoons vanilla extract

5 quarts water

PREPARATION IN CAMP:

1. Mix sugar, cocoa powder, salt, cinnamon, powdered milk, and vanilla extract in a large cook pot.
2. Add water and bring to a boil for about 2 minutes.
3. Lower heat to a simmer then serve in mugs.

REQUIRED EQUIPMENT:

Large cook pot (at least 8-quart capacity)

Beverly Jo Antonini, Morgantown, West Virginia
Assistant Scoutmaster
Troop 49, Mountaineer Area Council

Servings: 20 (about 8 ounces each)
Preparation Time: ¼ hour
Challenge Level: Easy

Order of the Arrow Spiced Tea

7 quarts water

2 cups Tang powdered drink mix

4 cups granulated sugar

2½ cups unsweetened instant tea powder

2 teaspoons ground cinnamon

1 teaspoon ground cloves

½ teaspoon salt

"The months of January, February, and March are special at our camp for the Order of the Arrow youth and adults. We usually have snow, and the boys come in cold and wet. This is one of the hot drinks I like to have ready for them."

PREPARATION AT CAMP:

1. Boil water in large cook pot.
2. Mix the dry ingredients together in a medium-size bowl then stir into boiling water.
3. Remove spiced tea from the heat and stir until ingredients are dissolved.
4. Serve in mugs.

REQUIRED EQUIPMENT:

Large cook pot (at least 10-quart capacity)
Medium-size mixing bowl

Beverly Jo Antonini, Morgantown, West Virginia
Assistant Scoutmaster
Troop 49, Mountaineer Area Council

Servings: 32 (about 8 ounces each)
Preparation Time: ¼ hour
Challenge Level: Easy

Sweet Sun Tea

2 gallons (8 quarts) water

16 (family-size) bags regular black tea

Optional flavorings (choose one): Fresh mint leaves; 1 orange, sliced into thin rounds; 1 lemon, sliced into thin rounds

3 cups granulated sugar or honey

Ice

PREPARATION AT CAMP:

1. Pour water into a 2-gallon clear covered jar or container and add tea bags along with any optional ingredients.
2. Place jar in direct late-morning to early-afternoon sunlight.
3. Allow jar to sit in the sun for at least 3 hours or until tea reaches desired strength.
4. Add sugar or honey and stir.
5. Serve over ice.

REQUIRED EQUIPMENT:

Clear covered jar or container with at least 2-gallon capacity

Option: This recipe is easily adaptable to any kind of tea in bags. If substituting herbal or green tea, use 4 regular-size tea bags for each family-size bag.

Tim Conners, Statesboro, Georgia
Assistant Scoutmaster
Troop 340, Coastal Empire Council

Christine Conners, Statesboro, Georgia
Committee Member and Merit Badge Counselor
Troop 340, Coastal Empire Council

Who needs a stove to brew tea when you have the sun? *CHRISTINE CONNERS*

TIP: For quick, clean removal of the tea bags, do not allow any tea bag labels at the end of the strings to fall into the jar.

Servings: 32 (about 8 ounces each)
Preparation Time: 3 hours
Challenge Level: Easy

Four-Seasons Punch

1 (12-ounce) can frozen orange concentrate, thawed

1 (12-ounce) can frozen lemonade concentrate, thawed

1 (64-ounce) container pure grape juice

1 (64-ounce) container pure pineapple juice

2 cups granulated sugar

4 quarts water

For hot punch only: 2 cinnamon sticks

For cold punch only: ice

PREPARATION AT CAMP:

FOR HOT PUNCH:

1. Combine juices, sugar, water, and cinnamon sticks in a large cook pot.
2. Barely bring punch to a boil then remove from heat.
3. Serve in mugs.

FOR COLD PUNCH:

1. Combine juices, sugar, and water in a large container.
2. Fill remaining space in the container with ice and allow to chill before serving.

REQUIRED EQUIPMENT:

For hot punch only: large cook pot (at least 10-quart capacity)
For cold punch only: large container (at least 10-quart capacity)

Tim Conners, Statesboro, Georgia
Assistant Scoutmaster
Troop 340, Coastal Empire Council

Christine Conners, Statesboro, Georgia
Committee Member and Merit Badge Counselor
Troop 340, Coastal Empire Council

Servings: 35 (about 8 ounces each)
Preparation Time: ¼ hour
Challenge Level: Easy

Appendix A

COMMON MEASUREMENT CONVERSIONS

United States Volumetric Conversions

1 smidgen	$\frac{1}{32}$ teaspoon
1 pinch	$\frac{1}{16}$ teaspoon
1 dash	$\frac{1}{8}$ teaspoon
3 teaspoons	1 tablespoon
48 teaspoons	1 cup
2 tablespoons	$\frac{1}{8}$ cup
4 tablespoons	$\frac{1}{4}$ cup
5 tablespoons + 1 teaspoon	$\frac{1}{3}$ cup
8 tablespoons	$\frac{1}{2}$ cup
12 tablespoons	$\frac{3}{4}$ cup
16 tablespoons	1 cup
1 ounce	2 tablespoons
4 ounces	$\frac{1}{2}$ cup
8 ounces	1 cup
$\frac{5}{8}$ cup	$\frac{1}{2}$ cup + 2 tablespoons
$\frac{7}{8}$ cup	$\frac{3}{4}$ cup + 2 tablespoons
2 cups	1 pint
2 pints	1 quart
1 quart	4 cups
4 quarts	1 gallon
1 gallon	128 ounces

Note: Dry and fluid volumes are equivalent for teaspoon, tablespoon, and cup.

International Metric System Conversions

Volume and Weight

United States	Metric
¼ teaspoon	1.25 milliliters
½ teaspoon	2.50 milliliters
¾ teaspoon	3.75 milliliters
1 teaspoon	5 milliliters
1 tablespoon	15 milliliters
1 ounce (volume)	30 milliliters
¼ cup	60 milliliters
½ cup	120 milliliters
¾ cup	180 milliliters
1 cup	240 milliliters
1 pint	0.48 liter
1 quart	0.95 liter
1 gallon	3.79 liters
1 ounce (weight)	28 grams
1 pound	0.45 kilogram

Temperature

Degrees F	Degrees C
175	80
200	95
225	105
250	120
275	135
300	150
325	165
350	175
375	190
400	205
425	220
450	230
475	245
500	260

British, Canadian, and Australian Conversions

1 teaspoon (Britain, Canada, Australia)	approx. 1 teaspoon (United States)
1 tablespoon (Britain, Canada)	approx. 1 tablespoon (United States)
1 tablespoon (Australia)	1.35 tablespoons (United States)
1 ounce (Britain, Canada, Australia)	0.96 ounce (United States)
1 gill (Britain)	5 ounces (Britain, Canada, Australia)
1 cup (Britain)	10 ounces (Britain, Canada, Australia)
1 cup (Britain)	9.61 ounces (United States)
1 cup (Britain)	1.20 cups (United States)
1 cup (Canada, Australia)	8.45 ounces (United States)
1 cup (Canada, Australia)	1.06 cups (United States)
1 pint (Britain, Canada, Australia)	20 ounces (Britain, Canada, Australia)
1 Imperial gallon (Britain)	1.20 gallons (United States)
1 pound (Britain, Canada, Australia)	1 pound (United States)

Equivalent Measures*

16 ounces water	1 pound
2 cups vegetable oil	1 pound
2 cups or 4 sticks butter	1 pound
2 cups granulated sugar	1 pound
3½ to 4 cups unsifted confectioners' sugar	1 pound
2¼ cups packed brown sugar	1 pound
4 cups sifted flour	1 pound
3½ cups unsifted whole wheat flour	1 pound
8–10 egg whites	1 cup
12–14 egg yolks	1 cup
1 whole lemon, squeezed	3 tablespoons juice
1 whole orange, squeezed	⅓ cup juice

* Approximate

Appendix B

SOURCES OF EQUIPMENT

Bass Pro Shops
www.basspro.com
Bass Pro stocks a large line of kitchen gear perfect for car camping, including a wide array of Lodge Dutch ovens and accessories. Bass Pro stores are a good place to go to see the equipment firsthand before you buy.

Boy Scout Catalog
www.scoutstuff.org
BSA Supply carries an assortment of handy camp kitchen gear as well as Lodge camp Dutch ovens in a range of sizes.

Cabela's
www.cabelas.com
This retailer specializes as a hunting and fishing outfitter but also carries a wide selection of outdoor kitchen gear and cookware. Cabela's has dozens of large retail stores located throughout the United States and Southern Canada.

Camp Chef
www.campchef.com
Many cast-iron cookware accessories are available through Camp Chef. The company also markets their own line of aluminum and cast-iron Dutch ovens, frying pans, and other cookware.

Campmor

www.campmor.com

Campmor stocks a huge selection of general camping supplies, many of them valuable for rounding out your list of basic equipment for a remotely located camp kitchen, farther from the car, where lightweight and compact are important characteristics for your gear.

Chuck Wagon Supply

www.chuckwagonsupply.com

The range of cast-iron cookware and accessories at Chuck Wagon is truly impressive. This is a great site to compare different Dutch oven makes and models and to discover all those items that you didn't know you needed. If you are looking for the lighter weight of aluminum ovens, you'll find a nice selection here. Chuck Wagon also stocks other items of value in the large group setting, including, for instance, giant griddles, enormous coffee pots, and the like.

Costco

www.costco.com

This popular membership warehouse stocks servingware in package sizes perfect for large-group settings. Retail stores are located throughout North America.

Dutch Oven Gear

www.dutchovengear.com

Scouter Sami Dahdal is CEO of Sam's Iron Works and its sister company, Dutch Oven Gear. A master wrought-iron craftsman, Sam manufactures quality tables and accessories for camp Dutch ovens. Stop by the website to see his gear in action.

Lodge Manufacturing

www.lodgemfg.com

Founded in 1896, Lodge is the premier source of a large array of high-quality cast-iron cookware and related accessories. It is the only company that still manufactures its full line of camp cast-iron cookware in the United States.

MACA Supply

www.macaovens.com

MACA manufactures a wide range of very deep camp cast-iron Dutch ovens, including what must be the largest on the market: a monster sporting a lid 22 inches in diameter and weighing in at 160 pounds. This is the place to go if you are looking for Dutch ovens that can feed 100 people or more. MACA also makes oval-shaped ovens, useful for roasting birds and larger cuts of meat.

REI

www.rei.com

Like Campmor, REI carries a large array of gear useful for the remote camp kitchen. REI also stocks an assortment of cast-iron cookware and accessories by Lodge.

Sam's Club

www.samsclub.com

Sam's Club, like Costco, is a large membership warehouse. Sam's has hundreds of retail locations across the United States and stocks a wide range of servingware, kitchen supplies, and groceries in bulk package sizes.

Sport Chalet

www.sportchalet.com

Sport Chalet is a major outdoor recreation retailer in the Southwest United States. Like Bass Pro Shops, this is a good place to go to see camp kitchen gear, Lodge cast iron, and related accessories before making the purchase.

The Wok Shop

www.wokshop.com

You'll find a great selection of high-quality, rugged Asian cookware appropriate for the camp environment at The Wok Shop's online retail store.

Appendix C

ADDITIONAL READING AND RESOURCES

Books and Periodicals

***Beef Stew for 2,500: Feeding Our Navy from the Revolutionary War to the Present,* Rudy Shappee, South Jetty Publishing**

Think that your group is large? Try planning meals for an aircraft carrier crew, nearly 5,000 strong. The book's interesting stories describe how the challenge of cooking for so many people so far from civilization has been addressed and solved over the centuries. No, it's not about outdoor cooking, but many analogies can be drawn. And you'll enjoy perusing the handful of recipes, including the one from the title: beef stew that serves 2,500 people.

Chuck Wagon Supply Bookstore

www.chuckwagonsupply.com

This Dutch oven specialty shop has a great selection of books and posts a wealth of helpful information for those new to cast-iron cooking.

***Cooking,* Merit Badge Series, Boy Scouts of America**

Scouts interested in camp cuisine will naturally want to pursue the cooking merit badge on their way to Eagle. This booklet covers the basics of indoor and outdoor cooking, food safety and nutrition, and careers in the food service industry. Detailed cooking merit badge requirements are included.

Cook's Illustrated* and *Cook's Country

www.cooksillustrated.com and www.cookscountry.com

These outstanding periodicals from America's Test Kitchen turn common recipes into wonderful re-creations with minimum effort. Along the way, the reader learns how and why the recipes work. *Cook's Illustrated* explores fewer dishes but in more detail than *Cook's Country,* its sister publication, which comes in a larger format and full color. These are magazines for the home kitchen. But what you'll learn indoors will prove invaluable at camp.

Lodge Manufacturing Bookstore
www.lodgemfg.com
The preeminent manufacturer of camp cast-iron cookware, Lodge offers a wide range of books and DVDs focusing on recipes and cooking techniques at their factory outlet stores and on their website.

***On Food and Cooking: The Science and Lore of the Kitchen,* Harold McGee, Scribner**
This is an excellent resource for understanding the science behind cooking. When chefs decipher why recipes work the way they do, they become much more effective at adapting recipes in a pinch or creating new ones on the fly. Be forewarned: This is not a cookbook, much less an outdoor cookbook. But if science interests you, this book will too.

***The Scout's Outdoor Cookbook,* Tim and Christine Conners, Globe Pequot Press**
The founding title of the Scout's Cookbook series, this book puts more emphasis on the recipes and less on the method. All popular forms of camp cooking are represented. Over 300 recipes are included, many award-winning, and all provided by Scout leaders from across the United States.

***The Scout's Dutch Oven Cookbook,* Tim and Christine Conners, Globe Pequot Press**
Focusing on the art of camp Dutch oven cooking, this book delves into technique without skimping on the recipes. Dozens of Dutch oven experts from throughout Boy Scouts of America contributed over 100 outstanding and unique camp recipes, most for an average group size from 8 to 12, consistent with the standard troop.

For more recipes and information on outdoor cooking, an online search will reveal a wealth of other sources.

Informational Websites

Epicurious

www.epicurious.com

You won't find much on camp cooking at Epicurious. But if you're looking to hone your basic cooking skills and could use thousands of recipes for practice, this is a good resource.

Exploratorium

www.exploratorium.edu/cooking

Exploratorium makes cooking fun by putting emphasis on the science behind it. Even if you're not the scientist type, you'll enjoy this site. Quirky yet practical, recipes flow down the page with relevant science posted in the sidebar.

International Dutch Oven Society (IDOS)

www.idos.com

The mission of IDOS is to preserve the art of Dutch oven cooking. According to IDOS, they are the largest and most productive group of "black pot" enthusiasts in the world.

Leave No Trace (LNT) Center for Outdoor Ethics

www.LNT.org

The Center for Outdoor Ethics has been a leader and respected voice in communicating why and how our outdoor places require responsible stewardship. The LNT outdoor ethics code is becoming standard practice within Scouting. More information about the organization is available at their website, and specific information about outdoor ethics principles, especially as applied to cooking, can be found in Appendix D of this book.

Appendix D

LOW-IMPACT COOKING

"Leave a place better than you found it." A Scout hears that phrase innumerable times over the years. In fact, low-impact wilderness ethics has become a core principle within Scouting, the mastery of which is a requirement for rank advancement.

Early Scoutcraft emphasized skills for adapting the camp environment to suit the needs of the outdoorsman. But in more recent years, with increasing use and pressure on our wild places, the emphasis has rightfully shifted toward developing wilderness skills within the context of minimizing one's impact on the outdoors and others.

In fact, the Boy Scout Outdoor Code states:

> ***As an American, I will do my best to***
> ***Be clean in my outdoor manners***
> ***Be careful with fire***
> ***Be considerate in the outdoors***
> ***Be conservation-minded***

By conscientiously following the Scout Outdoor Code, we become better and more thoughtful stewards of our natural resources.

The Leave No Trace Center for Outdoor Ethics also provides a set of principles that are becoming increasingly well known and applied within Scouting. These align closely with the Scout Outdoor Code. The principles of outdoor ethics from Leave No Trace enhance those of the Scout Outdoor Code by providing additional detail on their application.

The seven core principles of Leave No Trace are:

1. Plan ahead and prepare
2. Travel and camp on durable surfaces
3. Dispose of waste properly
4. Leave what you find
5. Minimize campfire impacts
6. Respect wildlife
7. Be considerate of other visitors

Careful planning, especially with respect to food preparation, is critical to successfully following the principles of both the Scout Outdoor Code and Leave No Trace, all of which are touched on once at camp. When preparing for an upcoming outing, consider the following list of application points as you discuss food and cooking options with your fellow Scouts and Scouters.

Decide how you'll prepare your food.

Some methods of cooking, such as gas stoves and grills, create less impact than others, such as open fires. Low-impact principles are followed when using a camp Dutch oven with charcoal on a fire pan, provided that the pan is placed on bare soil or rock, and the coal ash is disposed of in a discreet and fire-safe manner.

When using open fire to cook, follow local fire restrictions and use an established fire ring instead of creating a new one. Keep fires small. Collect wood from the ground rather than from standing trees. To avoid creating barren earth, find wood farther away from camp. Select smaller pieces of wood, and burn them completely to ash. Afterward, be sure the fire is completely out, then scatter the ashes. Learn how to use a fire pan or mound fire to prevent scorching the ground and blackening rocks. Don't bring firewood from home to camp if the wood might harbor insects or disease harmful to the flora in your camp area.

Carefully select and repackage your food to minimize trash.

Tiny pieces of trash easily become litter. Avoid bringing small, individually packaged candies and other such food items. Twist ties and bread clips are easily lost when dropped. Remove the wrappers and repackage such foods into ziplock bags before leaving home; or use knots, instead of ties and clips, to seal bread bags and the like.

Metal containers and their lids, crushed beverage cans, and broken glass can easily cut or puncture trash sacks. Wrap them carefully before placing them in thin-wall trash bags. Minimize the use of glass in camp. Scan the camp carefully when packing up to ensure that no litter is left behind.

When cooking for large groups, it can be even more challenging to maintain a clean camp because of the additional trash that's generated. Have adequate garbage receptacles available at camp and enforce their proper use.

Minimize leftovers and dispose of food waste properly.

Leftover foods make for messier trash and cleanup. If poured on open ground, they are unsightly and unsanitary. If buried, animals will dig them up. Leftovers encourage problem animals to come into camp if not properly managed. Carefully plan your meals to reduce leftovers. And if any remain, share with others or carefully repackage and set aside in a protected place to eat at a later meal.

Dispose of used wash and rinse water (also called gray water) in a manner appropriate for your camping area. Before disposal, remove or strain food chunks from the gray water and place these with the trash. If no dedicated gray water disposal area is available, scatter the water outside of camp in an area free of sensitive vegetation and at least 200 feet from streams and lakes. Avoid excessive sudsing by using only the amount of detergent necessary for the job. Bring only biodegradable soap to camp.

Plan to protect your food, trash, and other odorous items from animals.

Consider avoiding the use of very aromatic foods that can attract animals. Store food, trash, and other odorous items where animals won't be able to get to them. Besides being potentially dangerous to the animal, and inconvenient for the camper, trash is often spread over a large area once the animal gains access. Follow local regulations regarding proper food storage.

Decide whether to avoid collecting wild foods.

Don't harvest wild foods, such as berries, if these are not plentiful in the area you're visiting. Such foods are likely to be a more important component of the local ecosystem when scarce.

These are only a few of the practical considerations and potential applications of the principles of the Scout Outdoor Code and Leave No Trace. Visit www.LNT.org for additional information and ideas.

They find a little bit of food scraps here and there and, next thing you know, they act like they own the place.

TIM CONNERS

Appendix E

RELATED RANK AND MERIT BADGE REQUIREMENTS

The following list summarizes all current Boy Scout merit badge requirements related to food preparation that can be accomplished by using the instructional material and recipes in *The Scout's Large Groups Cookbook.*

Keep in mind that rank and merit badge requirements are updated by BSA on a regular basis, and the identification numbers and details for these may change from those shown here. Regardless, the list will point you in the right direction and give a good picture of how this book can be used to satisfy the requirements specific to a given rank or badge.

Rank Advancement

Tenderfoot

3 Assist with preparing and cooking a meal for your patrol on a campout.

Second Class

2(d) Prepare tinder, kindling, and fuel for a cooking fire.

2(e) Discuss when it is appropriate to use a cooking fire. Discuss safety procedures when using a cooking fire.

2(f) Demonstrate how to light a fire.

2(g) Plan and cook one hot breakfast or lunch for yourself in camp over an open fire.

First Class

4(a) Help plan a patrol menu consisting of at least one breakfast, one lunch, and one dinner, two meals of which must be cooked.

4(b) Make a list showing the food amounts required to feed three or more boys and secure the ingredients.

4(c) Describe which pans, utensils, and other gear are required to cook and serve these meals.

4(d) Explain the procedures to follow in the safe handling and storage of perishable food products. Tell how to properly dispose of camp rubbish.

4(e) On a campout, serve as patrol cook and supervise an assistant in building the cooking fire. Prepare the meals from 4(a). Supervise cleanup.

Merit Badges

Camping (required for Eagle rank)

2 Learn and explain the Leave No Trace principles and Scout Outdoor Code. Plan how to put these into practice on your next outing.

4(b) Assist a Scout patrol or Webelos unit with menu planning for a campout.

6(b) Discuss the importance of camp sanitation and why water treatment is essential.

7(a) Make a checklist of patrol gear required for your campout.

8(c) Prepare a camp menu and explain how it would be different from a menu for a backpacking or float trip. Select recipes and make a food list for your patrol, planning for two breakfasts, three lunches, and two suppers. Discuss how to protect your food against bad weather, animals, and contamination.

8(d) Cook at least two of the meals from 8(c) in camp. Both cannot be from the same meal category (i.e., breakfast, lunch, or dinner).

10 Discuss how working through the requirements for this merit badge has taught you about personal health and safety as well as public health.

Chemistry

4(a) Cook an onion until translucent, and cook another until caramelized (brown in color). Compare the tastes to that of a raw onion.

Cooking

1(a) Describe the injuries that can arise while cooking.

1(b) Describe how meat, eggs, dairy products, and fresh vegetables should be stored, transported, and properly prepared for cooking.

3(a) Plan a menu for two straight days of camping (six meals total, consisting of two breakfasts, two lunches, and two dinners). One dinner must include a soup, meat, fish, or poultry, along with two fresh vegetables and a dessert.

3(b) The menu in 3(a) must include a one-pot dinner, not prepared with canned goods.

3(c) Make a list for the menu from 3(a) showing the food amounts required to feed three or more boys.

3(d) List the utensils required to prepare and serve the meals in 3(a).

4(a) Using the menu from 3(a), prepare for yourself and two others the two dinners, one of either lunch, and one of either breakfast. Time the cooking so that each course will be ready to serve at the proper time. The meals may be prepared during separate camping trips.

4(b) For meals prepared in requirement 4(a) for which a fire is needed, build a low-impact fire (use a backpacking stove to cook at least one meal).

4(c) For each meal in 4(a), use safe food-handling practices. Following each meal, dispose of all rubbish properly and clean the campsite thoroughly.

Fire Safety

10(b) Demonstrate setting up and putting out a cooking fire.

10(c) Demonstrate the proper use of a camp stove.

10(d) Explain how to set up a campsite safe from fire.

Fishing

9 Cook a fish that you have caught.

Fly Fishing

10 Cook a fish that you have caught.

Theatre

4(d) Mime or pantomime a situation in which you are at camp with a new Scout, trying to help him pass a cooking test, but he learns very slowly.

Discuss with your merit badge counselor how to best apply this book for the specific rank and merit badges you are working toward.

Index

ABOUT THE AUTHORS

Experienced campers, backpackers, and outdoor chefs, Tim and Christine Conners are the authors of *The Scout's Outdoor Cookbook, The Scout's Dutch Oven Cookbook, The Scout's Large Groups Cookbook,* and *The Scout's Backpacking Cookbook,* each a collection of unique and outstanding camp recipes from Scout leaders across the United States. Tim and Christine are also the authors of *Lipsmackin' Backpackin',* one of the most popular trail cookbooks of the past decade.

Tim and Christine have been testing outdoor recipes for over fifteen years now. At the invitation of Boy Scouts of America, the Conners have twice served as judges for *Scouting* magazine's prestigious national camp food cooking contest.

The Conners have four children, James, Michael, Maria, and David, their youngest. Tim is Assistant Scoutmaster and Christine is Committee Member and Merit Badge Counselor for the Coastal Empire Council's Troop 340 in Statesboro, Georgia, where their two oldest sons have attained the rank of Life Scout and are on the road to Eagle.

The Conners family stays busy in the outdoors by camping and day-hiking in the local state parks, backpacking on the Appalachian Trail, and kayaking on the region's lakes and rivers . . . when they aren't writing cookbooks.

Stop by www.scoutcooking.com to say howdy!

The Conners family shares dinner along the Appalachian Trail. *DAVID LATTNER*